SUCCESSFUL DEBT C

SUCCESSFUL DEBT COLLECTING

ANDREW BOGLE
Solicitor
Thelwell Fagan

and

JOHN FULLER
Chartered Accountant
Managing Director (formerly Finance Director)
Jordans

JORDANS
1996

Published by
Jordan Publishing Limited
21 St Thomas Street
Bristol BS1 6JS

British Library Cataloguing-in-Publication Data
A catalogue record for this book is available from the British Library.

ISBN 0 85308 323 1

Typeset by Mendip Communications Ltd, Frome, Somerset
Printed by Hobbs the Printers of Southampton

PREFACE

Cash-flow is the lifeblood of any organisation. Get it right and you have a healthy foundation on which to build. Get it wrong and all that hope and hard work may end up as just another statistic.

This book is about getting it right. It is geared to anyone who needs to know about credit control and pursuing action through the courts. Part I, by John Fuller, covers procedures to prevent outstanding invoices from turning into bad debts. Part II, by Andrew Bogle, takes the reader through typical steps in a county court action.

The language used is simple and direct. There are many practical examples including how to complete standard court forms and how to conduct common hearings. More parties in person appear in the courts each year. This book is designed to assist them in presenting their case in the best possible light.

The procedures shown are those of the county courts located throughout England and Wales. Scotland and Northern Ireland have their own courts with different procedures.

To the best of the authors' belief *Successful Debt Collecting* is an accurate statement of the law and practice as at March 1996. Be warned though; the law does change and a far-reaching review of civil litigation procedure by the Lord Chancellor's Department continues.

The pronouns 'it' and 'he' have been used as appropriate to suit the particular circumstances when referring to the Plaintiff and the Defendant.

ANDREW BOGLE
JOHN FULLER
April 1996

CONTENTS

PART I

PREVENTION

Chapter 1

THE BUSINESS OF DOING BUSINESS

1.1 Risk

Traditional views suggest that a business exists for the sole benefit of its proprietors who are risking their own capital to secure a financial return. However, in these more enlightened times, it is considered that businesses have a responsibility to a range of 'stakeholders' who would expect to derive benefit from its activities. These include not only proprietors but also staff, customers and the wider community. For most people, being in business usually involves taking risks, and businesses will spend a lot of time and money trying to minimise the risk to a level at which all the stakeholders can sleep at night. Successful businesses are those which can maximise their return while minimising risk.

Under this more modern definition of a business's wider responsibilities, customers are one of the groups who should derive benefit from the business. However, it is not the intention of this book to suggest that customers should benefit at the expense of the business by not paying their debts to the business but rather that the business should seek to provide quality services and products for which the customers happily pay on time.

To achieve this, a business must have in place effective means of credit control and debt collection. This is equally relevant to non-profit-making organisations, such as charities, clubs or government bodies, as it is to profit-making concerns. This book is therefore of interest to all kinds of organisations where goods or services are bought and sold.

1.2 Cash-flow

Apart from the obvious stakeholder risks inherent with being in business, the greatest practical risk that any business faces is failure to generate cash. There have been a number of highly publicised cases (and many more lesser known ones) where businesses have collapsed in spite of making profits. The explanation for this is the main message of this book: 'profit is only real when it is in the bank'.

It does not matter how profitable a business is on paper, if it does not generate cash, it will not survive. It is worth noting that many struggling businesses have reported accounting losses for years but have survived by turning working capital into cash. This will keep the creditors (often the bank) from the door by 'buying' time to turn the losses into profits again. Often the most productive way of generating the necessary cash is by ensuring that customers pay for the goods and services they have bought and that they pay on time.

In other words 'cash is king'. Generating cash is, however, easier said than done and requires not only having the right product or service, in the right place, at the right time, and at the right price, but also having a buyer who pays on time. Clearly, even the best run business which has got all these factors right will still fail if it does not understand the importance of getting the money owed to it from its customers and getting it into the bank.

It is also important to understand what effect delayed payment by customers will make to the business. While Part II of this book deals with the legal processes for recovering debt (the ultimate cash-flow problem of non-payment of debts), Part I of this book is concerned with getting paid and getting paid on time. Delays in collecting debts can have as serious an effect on a business as ultimate non-payment of debts, particularly if a large number of customers is involved. Slow customer payment is a common problem and can mean the difference between a business surviving or failing.

Evidence suggests that the customers most likely to delay payment are large business customers who have a deliberate policy of slow payment to assist their own cash-flow but at the expense of the smaller businesses to whom they owe money. Part I of this book will show how to turn the tables.

1.3   Inflation

The cash-flow problem discussed above is multiplied exponentially when the effects of inflation are also taken into account, as shown in the following very simple example.

A business which has sold goods to the value of £20,000 can buy with that money two essential services priced today at £5,000 and £15,000 respectively. Let us assume that the business is unable or unwilling to borrow money to buy these services and that they can only therefore be secured once the business has been paid the £20,000 it is owed by its customer (the supplier of these services has already read this book and is demanding cash in advance!). If the customer pays immediately, then the business will have sufficient money to buy the services. However, if the customer pays after three months (which is not uncommon) and during that time inflation has increased the cost of the essential services required to £5,100 and £15,300, making a total of £20,400, the business can no longer afford to pay for these services out of the proceeds of its earlier sales. The fact that the customer failed to pay on time means that the business has lost money.

1.4   Pricing and inflation

The situation described above is self-perpetuating. In that example, the business will now have to make an allowance in its pricing for the fact that the customer will take three months to pay and, consequently, it will have to put up the price for its goods to £20,400. This will, in turn, add to inflationary pressure on its own customers, and an inflationary spiral will have been created simply because of this three-month delay in payment.

We are not suggesting that this book provides an answer to inflation (although if the Chancellor were to take some action on the trade debt problem, he might be pleasantly surprised to find that it would help to control inflation and at the same time support the small businesses which are so important to the economy). Our intention in this book is to demonstrate the impact on a business of customers not paying on time and how important it is for long-term survival to reduce this risk to a minimum.

1.5   Outside help

The purpose of this book is to provide a self-help route to successful debt collection. However, it would be wrong to suggest that this task cannot involve the help of others. One obvious form of help would be to employ a solicitor to deal with the legal processes, which are set out in Part II. However, the main aim of this book is to assist those who would prefer to handle the debt collection process themselves. Instead, we refer here to some of the sources of outside help which can reduce the burden of credit control and debt collection, release value to the business for the money tied up in trade debt or limit the risks of dealing with unreliable customers.

Let us take each briefly in turn.

1.5.1   Collection agencies

There are a number of agencies which are in the business of undertaking some or all of the routine credit control functions. Most of them are remunerated by results, which means that their costs can be related to the actual level of debt collected. The way these agencies work is by dealing with routine chasing, making use of computer-generated letters, then following up the letters with a telephone chasing regime. How this process will work is generally agreed at the outset, but it is then managed by the agency until collection is achieved or the decision is taken to pursue the debt through the courts. Most agencies will also offer a legal service. These agencies can perform a useful and effective role but care should be exercised over their use depending on the type of business and how important it is to maintain good relationships with customers during any potentially difficult period of chasing. Some agencies employ tough telephone tactics and are perhaps less concerned than the business with ongoing customer relations. That having been said, the fact that the agencies are independent often helps them to achieve good results.

1.5.2   Factoring or invoice discounting

There are a number of ways of factoring, but essentially it is a method by which money owed to a business by its debtors is 'sold' to a bank or specialist factoring house which pays the business a percentage of the value of the debt and then takes responsibility for collecting the whole debt from the debtor. The factoring company makes its money by keeping the difference between the amount it collects and the amount paid to the business. Factoring can be a very good way of releasing working capital from a business to enable it to expand rather than having to raise finance in other ways. The factoring services available range from simple cash discounting through to full sales ledger accounting. The discount rates vary considerably depending on the extent of service provided and the level of risk assumed by the factoring company.

1.5.3   Credit insurance

A business can pay a premium to an insurance company which will then insure it against non-payment by its debtors. This type of insurance grew up in the exporting market when the government-backed Exports Credit Guarantee Department was established to encourage UK business to venture into the world of exporting. It still tends to be a specialist area and is likely to be prohibitively expensive to the average business, particularly as the insurance company will be very selective about the debts that it is prepared to cover and is not likely to cover the potentially bad ones. A useful source of further information on this subject would be a local Chamber of Commerce.

1.6   The real world

Risk, as used in the context of this book, would be eliminated if a business could always get its customers' money in the bank before the goods or services are released to the customer. For those rare businesses where this occurs, there is no need to read further. In the real world, however, unless a business deals in cash in advance only, there is always some risk of not getting paid, and as this applies to the majority of businesses, large and small, read on.

Chapter 2

PREVENTION IS BETTER THAN CURE

2.1 Limit the risk

If the provision of credit is unavoidable in the day-to-day running of a business, it is vital that the necessary steps are taken to reduce to a minimum the risk of not getting paid. Most of this book is devoted to what should be done if all reasonable steps have failed. Part I deals with how to prevent debts arising in the first place; Part II deals with how to recover debts if all else fails. The objective of Part I, however, is to obviate the need for the steps contained within Part II.

2.2 Is it necessary to offer credit?

Offering credit to customers is a standard business practice. However, it is offered at the discretion of the management of the business and may depend upon the particular type of business operation. Most customers will prefer to pay on some type of credit arrangement rather than paying in advance of receipt of goods or services, and customers often assume credit is available unless they are told otherwise. Before any credit arrangements are offered, a business should carefully assess the impact that offering credit will have upon the business overall.

A good starting point is to study competitors directly or contact relevant trade associations to establish what payment terms are generally offered in similar businesses. In most areas of business, the market will have its own expectations. However, the credit arrangements offered by other businesses should be regarded only as a guide. Every business is unique and whilst it may be critical to the success of a business to be able to compete on equal terms with other similar businesses, it is also important to bear in mind the specific circumstances of a business as well as the type of customers the business will attract.

2.3 Establish a policy

To offer credit to customers and then to manage 'credit control', it is essential to establish a policy which is effective and efficient and to ensure that all the relevant personnel within the organisation are aware of this policy, and understand the part they play in it.

Establishing a policy will help your staff to deal with customers in a professional and efficient manner. By avoiding confusion among customers and staff it will help to reduce the risk of incurring late payment or non-payment of debts.

A well-planned policy will help to create good relationships with customers, especially if it encourages staff to be helpful and courteous, which in turn will generate more business.

The policy should cover the following:

- the granting of credit facilities;
- credit terms;
- credit limits;
- methods of debt collection;
- responsibilities within the organisation.

Most of these are general policy issues and will depend upon the requirements of the specific organisation, for example its size and type of business. Some of the practical implications of these issues are covered in Chapter 3.

One point which is dealt with in more detail here is setting credit limits, which may be set at different amounts for different customers and is a matter of personal judgement as to the credit worthiness of each customer, ie their ability to pay.

2.3.1   Credit limits

The amount of credit given to each customer should be determined as a monetary amount, for example £1000, and should then be recorded against the customer's account as their 'credit limit'.

A decision should be taken as to whether to disclose to customers their individual credit limits. This decision should also be recorded against the customer's account so that it is clear whether such sensitive information may be disclosed or not.

There are advantages and disadvantages with both options and, again, the most appropriate option will depend upon the specific business or specific customer.

If a customer knows and accepts the credit limit he is given at the outset, it is usually easier to tackle the situation if the credit limit is later exceeded, at which point the business must decide whether to stop any further credit until the unpaid bills are settled, or to extend the credit limit.

However, some customers may take advantage of their knowledge of their credit limit to delay payment until the limit is reached. One way to overcome this problem is to set two limits: a true limit which is not disclosed to the customer and which reflects the amount of risk the business is prepared to accept before any action will be taken; and a lower limit which is the amount of credit the customer is told he can have before his account will be stopped. However, setting two limits can in itself cause complications. Credit limits are discussed further in Chapter 3.

2.4 Knowing the customer

If a business, or an individual, approaches a bank for a loan or an overdraft, the bank will require detailed financial information about the applicant to assess whether to provide the loan or not. It is also common practice for a bank to take out credit references against an applicant as further security for the bank in protecting itself for the amount of the loan. This practice is widely known and expected.

Why then should the provision of credit to a business customer be any different? Yet it often is. On the one hand, customers usually expect credit to be provided automatically and do not expect questions to be asked about their credit worthiness. On the other hand, businesses rarely do ask questions before providing credit. Consequently, many businesses run into debt collection difficulties.

Accordingly, it is sound business practice in the provision of credit to find out as much as possible about a customer before any credit is offered.

Many businesses are embarrassed to ask the questions they need to ask, even though customers are not embarrassed to ask the business for credit. No business should put itself at risk in this way. It is vital for the health of any business to find out as much as possible about its customers to protect itself from unpaid debts. A polite yet confident approach to this will help create a good relationship with the customer at the outset.

It is in any event sound business practice to have some basic customer information for purposes other than debt collection. The information gathered will provide essential data for marketing new products and services as well as the data needed for customer accounting.

2.5 Getting the basics right

Often it is the basic information which proves to be the most important: the customer's name, address and telephone number. This information should be held on file and kept up to date along with any other contact names. Letters and items such as purchase orders should also be kept on file. Where the customer is itself a company, the customer's letterhead will provide the full company name, its registration number and registered office and, in some cases, the names of the company's directors, all of which information it is useful to have ready access to if any problems arise. For unincorporated businesses, it is useful to have the name of the proprietor or partners. If the company is part of a group of companies, it is also useful to know the names and addresses of the parent company or other offices or associates. Having all this information on file can mean the difference between collecting an outstanding debt quickly and, perhaps, in extreme cases, having to write it off completely because the customer cannot be traced. Chapter 4 deals with this in more detail.

2.6   Further information

It may be the case that basic information will be sufficient to decide what credit facilities can be offered to a customer. For example, a well-known 'blue chip' company whose credit worthiness is assured would be a reasonable credit risk. However, it is always wise to err on the side of caution and make some further investigations.

Any reputable customer should be willing to provide the information needed. A disreputable customer is more likely to be evasive. Whilst first impressions are important, beware of those customers who set out deliberately to deceive. The overall presentation a customer gives, together with the size of his company or the value of his account, can count for a lot but no one should trust these factors alone. There are many instances of apparently legitimate businesses trading fraudulently at the expense of their suppliers, so, in addition to the information the customer provides himself, it is worth seeking some third party information about the customer's trading record. There are several potential sources for this kind of information, some of which will be more time-consuming and possibly more costly to find than others.

2.6.1   General sources

Two common sources of information are bank and trade references. The customer should be willing to supply the name and address of his 'trading' bank and/or one of his own suppliers so that references, in writing, can be obtained from these sources. However, references of this kind are not infallible and can only be used as an indicator of a customer's trading status. They should certainly not be taken as guarantees. In most cases, bank and trade references are useful for finding out if the customer is a particularly bad risk and, if so, it is to be hoped that the information provided will be sufficient to determine the level of risk. However, sometimes only vague reference to the customer's financial standing and payment history is provided, which is insufficient for the business to decide whether to risk its capital by offering credit. To find out more, the business should contact its own bank.

Trade associations are another useful source of information. Check whether the customer is a member of a trade association, which is often shown on the customer's letterheading, and contact them direct. Again, this can only be a guide but it will identify whether a customer is a genuine member of that association and whether there have been complaints made against them. However, it will not identify whether they are bad payers of their debts or if they are likely to get into financial difficulty.

Another possible line of enquiry are quality assurance agencies such as the British Standards Institute. Many businesses are registered with these agencies to demonstrate their commitment to quality in their market. Check if the customer is registered with any of these agencies, which will at least indicate whether the customer is concerned with quality systems which include supplier systems and, if necessary, contact the relevant agency for assurances that the customer is meeting their quality standards.

2.6.2 Credit references

For more detailed information, make use of the various business information providers and credit reference agencies (eg Jordans, CCN). The level and type of information available will depend on whether the customer is a limited company, an unincorporated business or an individual. Most business information providers are able to supply detailed information on limited companies based on the accounts and other documents which companies must file with Companies House. Subject to the size of the company under investigation, it is possible to obtain its profit and loss account, its balance sheet, details of any charges that have been lodged against it, whether any winding-up petitions have been filed, who the directors and shareholders are, etc. In addition, for non-limited companies, a credit reference agency will be able to provide an indication of credit worthiness based on the information held on its database which is collected from a number of different sources such as credit card issuers and loan companies.

The extent of any search for information should be related to the level of credit and potential risk to which the business will be exposed. Our advice would be to take the time and trouble to get to know the customer before undertaking any risk.

2.7 Obtain advance payment

The single most effective way to reduce risk is to obtain payment before undertaking to supply any goods or services. Payment may take a number of forms ranging from a percentage deposit, through stage payments (for longer-term work), to full payment in advance. Some of these methods are more common than others depending on the custom and the general practice within the specific market. It is quite common, for instance, for builders to require a deposit in advance to cover the cost of initial materials, and stage payments during the job to cover completed work. Some retailers will ask for full payment in advance where they are having to place an irrevocable order for goods that they would not normally stock.

As with most things in life, what you don't ask for, you don't get!

2.8 Make payment easy

Whether offering credit or asking for advance payment, do everything possible to make it easy for the customer to pay. Be prepared to accept a number of payment methods, such as cash, cheque, charge card, credit card or direct payment into the business bank account by standing order, direct debit or credit transfer, if they are relevant to the nature of the business. It may be worth considering differential pricing for certain payment methods depending on the cost of this to the business.

If customers are likely to want to pay by direct credit transfer into the business bank account, make sure that the customer is given all the relevant details in an easily located place, such as on customer invoices or statements. These details should include the full address of the bank branch, its sort code number, the name in which the account is held and the account number.

The risk associated with some payment methods can be further limited by making use of such facilities as telephone clearance of credit card payments, cheque guarantee cards, cheque clearance services, etc. The bank will be a willing source of help on such matters.

2.9   Do not provide scope for delay or query

The experienced slow payer (or non-payer) may employ a number of methods to make life difficult in collecting payment. It is up to the business to ensure that the opportunity for a customer to delay payment is eliminated or at least reduced to a minimum. Many of the ploys that are used are basic and simple, but are still surprisingly successful despite the fact that they may be avoided by equally simple means.

In the first place, ensure that you know what the customer wants and that he knows what he will get. Customers can and do (wittingly or unwittingly) ask for the wrong thing or say that what has been supplied is not what they asked for. In both cases, the outcome is potential non-payment. Try to obtain written confirmation of the customer's order. Ensure that the customer's requirements have been fully understood and, if there is any ambiguity, clarify his requirements before proceeding. If there is no written purchase order, then write to the customer confirming what it is that they have ordered and what will be supplied.

As mentioned earlier, there is no substitute for good record-keeping and when it comes to debt collection, this applies to both administrative and accounting records. The professional slow payer will exploit any weaknesses to the full. Poor records will also make life much harder when it comes to resolving genuine issues and misunderstandings with regular customers.

The key to good record-keeping is simplicity, accuracy and being up to date. If the records are well kept, customer queries can be answered quickly and simply, which will not only impress the customer and help to generate more business, but will also demonstrate to any disreputable customers that they are not dealing with amateurs.

2.10   Define the terms of business and terms of payment

Clearly defined terms of business and terms of payment serve two purposes. First, they explain to customers, in precise terms, the general conditions required by the business, and provide the customer with clear rules on payment periods. The second, connected, purpose arises when these terms of business are invoked as a way of recovering money owed by a non-payer. This is dealt with later in the book; at this stage, we will concentrate on defining the terms of payment.

The golden rule is to ensure that payment terms and methods are clear and easy to follow. Poorly worded terms will be exploited as yet another excuse for delayed payment. If invoices are due for payment immediately on raising or, say, 30 days from the invoice date, then this should be stated clearly on the invoices and on any statements which are sent out. The best practice is to inform all customers of payment terms at the outset. This can be achieved in a friendly introductory letter to new customers, welcoming their business and at the same time outlining the accounting terms and procedures (see sample letter at the end of this chapter). This letter can also be an opportunity to let customers know the different ways in which they can pay. Another opportunity to remind customers of payment terms is to send a letter of confirmation of their order. This is particularly relevant if there are different payment terms for different types of products or services as it enables you to be specific in relation to each order.

The Government has been under increasing pressure from the business community to introduce statutory help to try to reduce the problem of slow payment of trade debt. Many EC countries have such statutory provisions, but the UK Government has been reluctant to follow suit, concentrating instead on offering relief against the loss of VAT on bad debts rather than limiting the problem before it reaches the bad debt stage (treating the symptoms at the expense of finding a cure). The main weapon used elsewhere is the right to charge interest on overdue payments and, although there is no statutory help in the UK (unless a court judgment has been obtained), it may be worth considering putting some reference to interest charges in the terms of payment. This can either be done by stating that interest will be added to overdue payments (which can be difficult to enforce) or by offering some form of discount against the outstanding amount if it is paid within a certain period from the invoice date.

To a large degree, the payment terms that a business chooses will be influenced by the custom and practice in the particular market sector and what the business can afford (a high margin business can afford to be a little more generous with its credit terms than a low margin one). There is, however, little point in trying to set terms that are totally at odds with those generally accepted. The key is to set terms that can reasonably be expected to be enforced, otherwise they will work against the business as customers will ignore them and it will be even more difficult to impose any sort of routine payment pattern. It is necessary to be firm and sensible in setting the right payment terms for your business.

Welcoming letter

Dear Sirs

We are pleased to confirm that the following account has been opened for you:

Account name:	XYZ & Company
Address:	1, High Street, Anytown
Account number:	123456

Please will you check that your name and address and the account details are correct and notify us immediately of any necessary amendments.

For your reference, we enclose a copy of our terms and conditions of business which sets out, among other things, the way in which your account with us is to be operated and the penalties that may be invoked should the account fall into arrears.

When corresponding with us, it will be helpful if you always quote your account number. Should you at any time have cause for concern or complaint in respect of the service you receive, please do not hesitate to contact me personally.

We look forward to being of service to you.

Yours faithfully

Managing Director

Chapter 3

EFFECTIVE CREDIT CONTROL PROCEDURES

3.1 Technique

A good maxim to remember when it comes to effective credit control is that 'technique matters but sheer effort will get results'. There is no substitute for persistence and sheer determination when it comes to getting payment from customers and this chapter discusses the techniques which can be applied to help. However, the ultimate effectiveness of any credit control techniques will, to a large extent, depend upon how much resources a business is able or willing to devote to the activity. It should not be assumed that only large businesses, which have personnel dedicated to chasing customers for payment, need to have credit control procedures. Every business, small and large, should set up some form of procedure which it rigorously maintains.

3.2 Routine

To make best use of the resources available for credit control, it is necessary to establish routine procedures which are as simple as possible to carry out, but which produce results. But beware of the routines which can, by their very nature, allow the habitual slow payer to learn the procedures and exploit them by always delaying payment until the last possible moment, in the knowledge that the routines will permit this without serious consequence.

It is therefore very important regularly to review credit control procedures and their effectiveness, and perhaps vary tactics from time to time where the standard procedures have failed.

So what are these magic routines? Like many other aspects of running a business, they are largely common sense but they are the most frequently overlooked and underestimated areas of the business and can mean the difference between success and failure. No matter how well a business is run or how good its product or services are, if its customers do not pay their bills, the business will fail.

3.2.1 Stage 1: invoices

Some types of business involve raising invoices more frequently than others. It is up to the business to determine when invoices are raised, depending on whether it is more efficient to raise them on an order-by-order basis, weekly, monthly, etc. This may depend upon the volume of invoices and the value of each invoice. For example, a large number of low-value invoices might take longer to raise than a small number of high-value invoices so time should be allowed for this. However, the essential point to make is that whatever type of invoice the business raises, there must be a standard method whereby the goods or services supplied are invoiced and that suitable records are kept to ensure that everything supplied is accounted for. If a business fails to keep track of what a customer has received, it cannot hope to keep track of what it should charge or how much it is owed.

The first stage in the credit control procedure is to ensure that invoices to customers are raised at the earliest opportunity. Clearly, any delay will result in a later payment being made, which is a cost to the business. Where possible, send invoices at the time of despatch of the goods. For the supply of services, this may be more difficult especially where it is not clear when the service has been completed. If this is the case, then interim or stage invoices should be considered. If so, it would be wise to advise customers that interim invoices are company policy.

Always bear in mind that it is the point at which an invoice is raised which sets the whole process of collection in motion.

3.2.2   Stage 2: reminders

The second stage is to keep track of the due date for payment and send out reminders for all unpaid invoices. This can be in the form of a statement of account or a letter or both.

The due date for payment is at the discretion of the business but should be carefully considered and whatever period is decided, it should be rigidly pursued.

(a)   Statements

Generally, a statement of account is the first reminder following an invoice. Statements are best sent to every customer on a monthly basis. If, for example, the due date for payment is 30 days after the invoice date, then the end of each month will be an appropriate point in the cycle to issue a statement.

Statements are best issued at a fixed point in the month, for example on the last day of each month, and this should be strictly adhered to.

Make use of the statement to check how much is owing each month and how long overdue it is. Analyse the age of the balance due and base this ageing on the payment terms so that it clearly shows the amount overdue for payment. Try highlighting the statement with red stickers to bring the customer's attention to the overdue balance. Put as much detail as possible on the statement about each individual invoice to help identify them without having to refer back to the invoices. This will prevent the customer from trying out a common ploy in the slow payment game: asking for copy invoices, a ploy which is designed to delay payment further. If, at the outset, the statement includes adequate detail to identify the precise goods or services supplied, there is less scope for the customer to try to delay payment by claiming he does not know what the payment requested is for. This might seem like a minor point but it can help reduce the excuses a customer can make to justify not paying on time.

(b)   Letters

Reminder letters are an essential part of the credit control procedure (see examples at the end of this chapter). As an alternative, or as back up to the statement of account, there should be a series of standard letters sent to customers starting from a polite yet firm reminder and leading progressively to a threat of court action. The sequence of reminder letters should not be spread out over too long a period of time and the letters should specify time-limits for payment and explain what will happen next if payment is not made. Whatever is said in these letters, it must be acted upon and rigorously followed up to ensure that the customer knows that what you say is what you mean.

The chosen routine for standard letters should include flexibility to take account of genuine reasons for non-payment but must also be tight enough to ensure that letters are sent out regularly and on time and followed up.

It is important that there is a written record of all communications to and from customers with regard to payment of invoices for two reasons:

(1)   so that a customer history is kept to help in future dealings with that customer; and
(2)   so that if a court action arises, there is clear evidence of events.

3.2.3   Stage 3: telephone calls

Just as telephone contact is often an essential element in winning a customer's business, it is equally important when trying to get paid. Where reminder letters can be ignored, a telephone call will force the unresponsive customer to address the problem. However, chasing money by such a direct approach can be a daunting prospect, but it is a very quick and effective way to find out what you need to know before taking any further action. The busy customer may even welcome telephone contact to save valuable time rather than have to deal with piles of paperwork, and a telephone conversation may often reveal a reason for non-payment which written contact would not, for example a death in the family, holiday absence etc. This kind of knowledge can be invaluable in future dealings with a customer.

In any telephone contact with customers, it is generally advisable to be polite at all times, even if the customer forgets to be polite back. Whoever has responsibility for making debt-collecting phone calls should be able to handle the 'difficult' customer in a way which is both polite yet firm. It will be a wasted call if nothing is achieved other than frayed tempers which can do more harm to the customer relationship than good.

The secret is to be well informed about the current status of the customer's account before making the call in case the customer asks any questions about the account, and to be well prepared with the questions which you will need to ask the customer in order to get the information you require. Always bear in mind the precise reason for the call and make sure that the call is not terminated without getting that information. It is good practice to clarify what has been agreed before the call ends and to finish the call on polite terms. It will not help future relationships with the customer if all the customer remembers is being bullied.

Once a call has ended, it is also good practice to note in the customer records what has just been agreed so that there is a written record for the next stage of chasing.

If payment was promised by a certain date and it does not arrive, telephone again on the due date reminding the customer of what was previously agreed and continue this process as necessary. In this way, the telephone is a quick way to chase unpaid debts. Its effectiveness will depend on careful monitoring of what was discussed, whether it has achieved direct results or whether further action is needed.

3.3   Monitoring and statistical analysis

As outlined in Chapter 1, a significant part of running most businesses involves taking risks which in turn involves risk control. Risk control is generally about managing money and measuring in financial terms how well the business is doing. Credit control is an essential part of this risk management process ensuring that trade debts are converted into cash as quickly as possible in order to limit the risk of not getting paid at all.

Effective credit control relies upon accurate accounting procedures which will provide at any given point the necessary figures to analyse the current financial state of the business. Not only is this essential for ensuring that the account information being sent to customers is accurate and dependable for chasing purposes, but it will also provide the basis for calculating statistics which can be used to aid the control of trade debtors and the minimising of risk.

3.3.1   Credit limits

Setting credit limits, as discussed in Chapter 2, provides a useful means of monitoring individual customers' accounts and can help to trigger the next step in the credit control procedure when a credit limit has been reached. It is important to understand, however, that just because an account is within its credit limit does not mean that the account is alright. Any outstanding balance should be analysed, either on the monthly statements or the copy invoices, to determine how long overdue each item is even if the total monies outstanding are within the set credit limit. Hidden within an account which is operating within its credit limit could be a large outstanding amount which has been outstanding for a long time. The effect of this on the business could be a serious financial loss especially if several accounts are allowed to operate in this way. Always remember that unpaid bills cost the business money and this will be a great motivator to pursue outstanding debts.

As with all monitoring measures, credit limits are only a part of the overall picture, but they are a very important part as they represent the cash risk a business is prepared to take with each customer and the total risk the business is taking with all its customers.

Credit limits can be flexible. It may be sensible with a new customer account to restrict the credit limit until a measure of trust with the customer has been established and a pattern of trading has emerged. After a period of satisfactory dealings, the limit can then be reviewed and, if appropriate, extended to a more practical figure depending on the amount of activity in the account. This review process is an essential element of credit control and should be undertaken on a regular basis for all accounts. Do not be afraid to reduce a previously established credit limit if there is concern about a change in a particular customer's standing: the finances of the business are at stake.

3.3.2   Age analysis

The other essential method of credit control which can be applied both at individual account level and also across the total trade debt balance is age analysis. This is the process of looking at the age of the invoices that make up the balance; information which should be included on the statement of account sent to customers (see **3.2.2(a)**). Age analysis overcomes the shortcomings of using a credit limit only to monitor customer accounts by clearly showing how up to date the customer is in paying invoices. The age bands into which the balance is divided will depend on the payment terms of the business, but assuming that payment is due 30 days after the date of the invoice then it might be sensible to arrange the account into bands of, say, less than 30 days, 30 to 60 days, 60 to 90 days and over 90 days. The amounts that are past their due date and how overdue the accounts actually are will then be clearly visible. If age analysis is undertaken for all sales ledger accounts then the business will be able to obtain a breakdown of its total trade debt, which, over time, will enable the business to gauge the effectiveness of its credit control procedures.

3.3.3   Debtor days

Closely linked with age analysis is the calculation of 'debtor days'. This is a statistical figure which is usually calculated across the total trade debt balance, not at individual account level. The number of debtor days expresses the outstanding trade debt of a business as a proportion of its sales. A figure of 75 debtor days, for example, would mean that the total trade debt of a business was equivalent to the value of 75 days' sales. The formula for the calculation is as follows:

$$\frac{\text{total trade debt}}{\text{annual sales}} \times 365$$

Debtor days offers a simple method of monitoring the overall level of credit being taken by customers and the effectiveness of credit control over time. Surveys show that in the UK, customers offered typical 30-day terms will pay within 72 to 78 days (ie a 42- to 48-day delay). The calculation of debtor days can help the business to see where it sits compared to these sorts of surveys as well as to make comparisons within its own part of the market. A good approximation of competitors' debtor days can be obtained from their annual accounts.

These forms of statistical/financial measures can be adapted to meet the particular requirements of the business and are only limited by imagination. Having said that, it is better to put greater effort into collecting money rather than into computing statistics, although the ability of a few well-directed statistics to give an overall feel for the risks and effectiveness of the time spent on credit control should not be underestimated.

3.4   Firmness

After this brief foray into the world of statistics, let us come back to the issue of routine and expand on some of the factors already discussed concerning the regular chasing of customers for payment.

In many ways, the key to successful debt collection depends on whether the customer thinks that he can play the delaying game with the supplier. If he perceives the business as weak in this respect, the customer may take advantage; if he respects the business and its credit control procedures, he will pay up within a reasonable time. However, this does not condone the use of strong-arm tactics which are likely to make the customer look for a different supplier. How often have you heard of a salesman blaming his company's credit control department for the loss of an account by being too heavy handed? There is a fine balance to strike between being firm and being harsh. So, be firm but not harsh. Customers must know that the supplier means business when it chases for payment but they must also know what is expected of them. The customer may be dealing with a number of suppliers and also having to play the payment game with its own customers. Cash-flow is likely to be a problem for the customer as well. It is therefore necessary to be understanding but the business must also ensure that it gets what it wants – payment. This is best achieved by spelling out to each customer what he probably already knows but is trying to ignore:

- how much is outstanding;
- when payment is expected by; and
- what action is likely to be taken next if payment is not forthcoming (eg placing the customer's account on stop).

Make all this as simple as possible, even to the extent of telling the customer how and where to make the payment. It is reasonable to expect customers to know this already but don't forget the game plan: reduce the scope for excuses to a minimum, or, better still, eliminate it altogether. Stick by the deadline set for the next step to be taken and follow the action through. If the next step is to issue a summons after so many days with no further reference back to the customer, then do it. Regular customers will soon get to know that the supplier means business and, unless there is a genuine reason for non-payment, they are likely to pay up on time in future to avoid further action and possible additional costs (eg interest charges, collection fees, court costs, etc).

As with all steps in the credit control process, keep records. Keep copies of letters (either as photocopies or on disk) and make notes of telephone conversations showing dates and the agreed course of action. Don't be shy about using this information in subsequent follow-up letters or telephone calls: this is all part of convincing the customer that he will have to choose another supplier if he wants to play the delaying game.

3.5 Policies

It will be clear by now that much of the credit control process is to do with discipline. Sloppy credit control will be punished by overdue payment, lost cash-flow and lower profits (or even losses). Through rigorous adherence to a disciplined credit control process, a business can educate its customers to be disciplined in their payment routines. But this discipline must start in the office and must be understood and accepted by all staff involved in the process.

An excellent way of achieving this is to define the credit control policies and formally document them. This may seem somewhat bureaucratic but it works. The scope of the documentation will obviously depend on the size of the business and the extent of the credit control function, but even where the proprietor himself has to chase customers for payment, and the time available to devote to credit control is, out of necessity, limited, the discipline that documented procedures can bring is invaluable. Written policies will also help when discussing credit facilities with a new customer and will establish a suitably professional relationship with the customer right from the outset.

The policy document should be in two parts. The first part should set down the defined policy concerning the offering of credit, the setting of credit limits, payment terms and methods, what steps will be taken on overdue payments, etc. The second part should detail how the policy will be exercised in practice and should cover, for example, office routines, the required frequency of tasks, responsibilities, methods of communication and all the other day-to-day aspects that will need to be understood by all those involved in the credit control process to make it work successfully.

Finally, once the policy document has been compiled it is important to ensure that the policy is followed and that it is reviewed from time to time to keep it relevant to the changing circumstances of the business.

3.6 Problem customers

All businesses are at some stage bound to encounter the problem customer. Here, we are not concerned with the slow payer, for whom all of the techniques of this book may be required to secure payment, but rather the customer who is in financial difficulty and who, unless care is taken, will cost much more than is bargained for.

As with other parts of the credit control process, there are ways of minimising the impact of such situations by recognising as early as possible what type of customer is being dealt with. This is relatively easy when the customer has no previous track record with the business, because in the early days of a new account it is essential to establish some form of payment pattern and warning bells should ring if the account becomes overdue in this period. However, if a reliable, long-standing customer suddenly becomes a problem, the change of circumstance can easily catch the business out in a potentially costly way.

This is where statistical techniques and routine procedures can prove to be a life-saver. Careful monitoring of credit limits and payment patterns, age analysis and personal contact with the customer can all provide an invaluable early warning system of impending disaster. If disaster subsequently strikes then, unfortunately, no amount of sound procedure is likely to help: it becomes a question of damage limitation.

Damage limitation is all about the ability to recognise the signs of trouble in time to do something about it. Spotted early enough, it may be possible to discuss the situation with the customer and even find some way of helping the customer through a difficult patch. In this way, the probability of a lost account and non-payment of a current debt could be turned into the possibility of more business in the future if the customer's difficulties are resolved. Obviously, great care is required in preparing to enter into some form of arrangement with a customer in difficulty, but it does at least provide an opportunity to work out the problem.

When faced with a potential bad debt, it is often a case of first come first served: those creditors at the back of the queue may receive scant compensation. But if the business had a good relationship with the customer and dialogue takes place early enough (ie before matters are taken out of the customer's hands by, say, his bank), the customer may be inclined to limit the damage to the business at the expense of some of his other, less supportive, suppliers.

In such situations, it is, unfortunately, entirely up to the business concerned as to what route to follow, and no amount of advice can teach the right and wrong approach to take: each circumstance is unique. All that can be done here is to encourage vigilance for any signs of impending trouble, as early action will give the business the best chance of coping with any problems that may arise.

3.7   Automation

In this computerised age, there is much that can be done to ease the burden of office routine, and, fortunately, credit control, consisting as it does largely of methodical, accurate record-keeping, lends itself well to automation. The options available range from basic word-processing, keeping track of letters, making notes of telephone conversations, etc, to sophisticated accounting packages for the sales ledger.

It is beyond the scope of this book to go any deeper into the available accounting software but it is certainly well worthwhile for a business to investigate the subject, no matter how basic or complex its credit control function may be.

First reminder letter

Dear Sirs

Account number 123456
Account balance £500

We regret to note that the balance on your account with us is overdue for payment. Please will you give this matter your immediate attention and bring your account up to date by paying the outstanding balance.

Cheques should be made payable to:

ABC Limited

and sent to:

The Credit Controller
ABC Limited
The Street
Anywhere

If you have any queries concerning the above, please contact the undersigned without delay. You should be aware that if this amount remains overdue we may have no alternative but to place the account on stop until payment is received.

Yours faithfully

Credit Control Department

Second reminder letter

Dear Sirs

Account number 123456
Account balance £500

We wrote to you on .... to advise you that the above account was overdue for payment. To date the amount is still outstanding. As the account is considerably in arrears we must ask that payment is sent to us within the next SEVEN days.

Cheques should be made payable to:

ABC Limited

and sent to:

The Credit Controller
ABC Limited
The Street
Anywhere

If you are unable to pay by this date please contact us immediately.

Unless we receive payment, or hear otherwise from you, we will take formal steps to recover the debt. In the meantime we regret to advise you that your account has been put on stop.

Yours faithfully

Credit Control Department

Third reminder letter prior to action (see also Chapter 4). It is suggested that for greater impact, this letter is printed on red paper. It is designed to look like a legal proceeding, even though it is not.

**Notice of intention to take
Legal Action**

NOTICE

Take notice unless you make payment of this debt within 7 days **Legal Action** will be taken against you without further warning.

How to pay

Cheques should be made payable to:

    ABC Limited

and sent to:

    The Credit Controller
    ABC Limited
    The Street
    Anywhere

Under our terms and conditions of business we reserve the right to add interest to the debt.

Please quote the account number on this document or return it when making payment.

For ABC Limited

Director

DEBT COLLECTING CYCLE

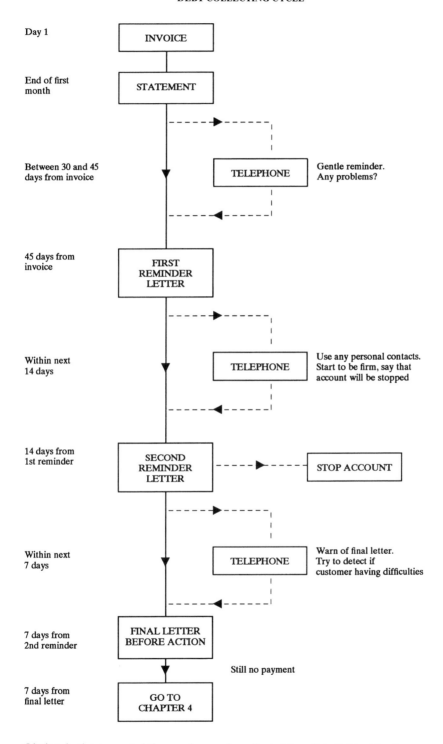

Obviously the suggested time scales can be adjusted to suit individual businesses.

PART II
CURE

Chapter 4

PREPARING FOR BATTLE

4.1   Preliminary steps

Where a customer is unable or unwilling to pay, the impetus must come from the creditor. The first steps are internal:

(1)   statements;
(2)   reminder letters;
(3)   telephone calls;
(4)   where appropriate, visits to the customer.

A contemporary record of discussions between the parties should be kept. If a customer states that he has cash-flow problems but will make payment in seven days this should be noted and confirmed by fax or letter, indicating the action which will follow should the customer default.

It seems incredible that some companies are prepared to continue to trade with customers following an earlier default in payment. There may be commercial considerations which dictate that everything should be attempted to preserve the business relationship but, once this breaks down, the only sensible course is to cease all future dealing.

4.1.1   Implementing repayment terms

A clear note of any delay or default in payment should be made on a customer's ledger. Checks should be made for any additional orders in the pipeline and halts placed on future work and delivery. It should be considered whether it is appropriate to invoke a retention of title clause (see further **4.4.2**). It should be ascertained if there has been contra-trading. If money is owing to the defaulting customer, settlement should be withheld. If the seller holds goods, plant or designs owned by the customer, these should be retained pending settlement of the overdue account; in each instance, a letter should be sent to the customer confirming the action being taken.

4.1.2   Establishing the existence and credit status of the debtor

Knowing the correct identity of a debtor is irrelevant if the debtor's whereabouts cannot be established and the debtor has no ability to pay. A creditor who satisfies himself on these two points prior to issuing proceedings will reduce the risk of wasting money.

The creditor should physically check that the debtor is still at the last known address. A telephone call may suffice, but visiting at the premises will give a clearer picture of the debtor's assets. A disconnected telephone or mail returned undelivered are obvious danger signs. It would be foolhardy to do business with a customer only prepared to provide a post office box number. A trading address should always be required.

If the debtor has left its last known address, how can its current whereabouts be traced? Trade connections may provide useful information, and certain public information is available. Creditors risk expending much time and effort attempting to track down a vanished debtor themselves, therefore, it is more efficient to instruct enquiry agents, placing a limit on their charges. They may have access to information not available to the general public. If they can trace the debtor, they may also be able to report on its financial status.

Beyond physical inspection of the debtor's premises, further information will be available regarding its financial position. Such information, however, will often be of limited application. By definition, the information is likely to be out of date. A better, if more expensive option would be to approach a credit reference agency. Such agencies provide a variety of reports, with additional information regarding the credit rating of a business.

4.1.3 Sources of information

When attempting to trace a debtor, consideration should be given to telephone and trade directories, trade federations, the Land Registry, the voters' roll and searches at Companies House for details of directors. Such information, however, may be out of date. The Driver and Vehicle Licensing Centre in Swansea should not divulge information, and the same applies to financial institutions and professional advisers.

Limited companies are obliged to file annual accounts. These, together with information including the officers of a company, its registered office, share capital, appointment of liquidators and receivers and debentures taken are available from Companies House. Company agents such as Jordans will provide such information at a fee. A telephone search available to subscribers at the Land Charges Department in Plymouth (telephone 01752 701171) will reveal if a bankruptcy petition has been issued against an individual.

A register of county court judgments is kept by the Registry Trust Limited, 173/175 Cleveland Street, London W1P 5PE. Postal searches cost £4.50. Advertisements of winding-up petitions, as well as publication of winding-up and bankruptcy orders and meetings of creditors appear in the *London Gazette*, published daily. A central registry of winding-up petitions issued is kept at the Royal Courts of Justice (telephone 0171 936 7328).

4.2 Who owes the money?

4.2.1 Identifying the debtor

A contract is entered into by two legal entities and identifying the debtor is not always as straightforward as might be imagined. Can the seller really be sure with whom it has contracted? One potential problem here is that pressure to obtain sales can undermine successful credit management. However, the benefit of securing further business for a company and benefits for the individual salesperson should never be at the expense of accurate information.

The credit manager needs to ensure that there are satisfactory procedures to correctly identify the debtor. The name and legal status of the party who is entering into the contract should be established, and whether he trades in an individual capacity. Alternatively, if the party is a partner in a firm, a credit manager should, if possible, obtain the full names and home, as well as business, addresses of the other partners. Failing this, he should discover at least the initials and surnames of the other partners and identify whether these individuals are male or female.

If an individual is contracting on behalf of a limited company, again, the credit manager should establish the full, correct name of that company and its registered office or principal place of business. If an individual is contracting on behalf of a club, charity or a body corporate, such as a local or health authority, it is necessary to establish its correct legal form. Where a party contracts as agent on behalf of a principal customer, credit procedures should ensure that full details of the principal against whom further action will follow are on file.

In addition to knowing the correct name and legal status of the debtor, a creditor must be able to prove that the debt exists. The debtor may deny having entered into a contract with the creditor or may operate under a variety of legal entities, either for legitimate business reasons or to create confusion. The contract may be oral, in writing, or a combination of the two. In the UK, there is no particular magic attached to a written contract. Except for sale of land, an oral contract is valid. The difficulty can be in proving who said what. Where it is one person's word against another, the potential area of dispute can multiply and any contested action becomes that much more problematic. Therefore, whenever possible, the details of contracts agreed orally should be confirmed in writing immediately.

The contract documents should be retained as these will assist in identifying a debtor. There may be a request for an estimate, an order confirmation, letter heading, cheques, details on references, a calling card or a signed proof of delivery. All can help in varying degrees. Sales representatives should not be satisfied with a trading name. If, for instance, a debtor is a limited company, trading as 'Law Books', it must be identified as such, preferably adding the trading name 'Law Limited t/a Law Books'.

The credit control department should retain a customer profile comprising all essential information, including full name and legal status. This should be updated when any changes occur, for instance, when a customer previously trading as a firm sets up as a limited company.

4.2.2 Status of the debtor

Money remains owing to the creditor despite its efforts to obtain payment. Relevant information and evidence have been offered, but there are some further considerations before action is commenced. Full names and descriptions should be employed where possible. The various legal entities which may be pursued are summarised as follows:

(1)   an individual, who may trade in his own name or use a trading name;
(2)   a firm, comprising two or more individual partners;
(3)   a limited company, styled either 'Limited', 'Company Limited', 'Ltd Co', 'Ltd', 'Public Limited Company' or 'PLC'. There are also Welsh language requirements. The vast majority of companies are limited by shares, a few being limited by guarantee. Foreign companies can be pursued where they have a principal place of business in England and Wales;
(4)   an unlimited company, although this type of entity is rare;
(5)   a charity. Details should be sought from the Charity Commission, St Albans House, 57 Haymarket, London SW1Y 4QX (telephone 0171 210 3000);
(6)   a club. An individual, firm or limited company may trade in this form. There are also members' clubs which must lodge details with the local authority. Action is taken against the officers of the club in their representative capacity. Careful investigation may be required;
(7)   a body corporate. This range of institutions includes local, health and education authorities. Again, care needs to be taken here.

Those entities which cannot be pursued in the courts include:

(1)   minors under 18 years of age and individuals covered by the mental health legislation who do not have the capacity to enter into contracts; and
(2)   an undischarged bankrupt. However, such a party will have committed an offence under the insolvency legislation.

The circumstances in which a creditor may, and why a creditor would want to, pursue a company in liquidation are discussed in Chapter 7. Where a person purports to contract on behalf of the company after it is placed in liquidation, a right of action will lie against that individual.

Where an individual with whom a creditor contracts, either on his own behalf or as a partner in a firm, then dies, a claim should be lodged with his estate and, if necessary, proceedings may be instituted against his executors or administrators. Searching and lodging caveats at the local Probate Registry may assist in identifying these individuals.

4.3   Information-gathering

4.3.1   In general

The importance of a well-documented case cannot be stressed too highly. The courts will not determine if a case is morally right and each claimant must prove that his is a valid claim. Certain basic documentation is required for undisputed claims. The value of being fully prepared will become apparent, however, when disputes arise. Credit controllers should ensure that the internal systems of their business are prepared for the possibility of future litigation and that essential documents are retained. A well-prepared case will always have a better chance of success.

The following points should be covered:

- contact carriers for proof of delivery;
- note terms and conditions of trading;
- note invoice due dates;
- does contractual interest apply?;
- obtain debtor bank account details;
- retain copies of cheques of untried customers.

Creditors should keep a separate file for each legal action, make a timed record of every telephone call, meeting or hearing and retain copies of any letter or document prepared.

It is worth noting that contractual interest is only available where there has been incorporated into the contract a provision for payment by a customer of interest at the given rate on overdue invoices. It may be difficult to satisfy the court that this term has been incorporated in the contract. Alternatively, if interest sought is excessive the defendant may claim the provision operates as a penalty at law and should not apply. Therefore, unless a creditor is confident that such arguments can be defeated, and the difference in rates claimed is significant, it may be preferable to claim statutory interest. (See also **6.2.1**).

4.4　Additional considerations

4.4.1　Notices of dishonour

Where a cheque has bounced, ensure that a notice of dishonour is sent in the following format.

> Dear Sirs,
>
> Account reference 5479
>
> TAKE NOTICE that the cheque drawn on account number 113333 of Jason Associates at Golden Fleece Bank of 123 Helen Street, Troy, dated 28th February 1995, in favour of Argonauts Ltd for £5,000 has been dishonoured on presentation. Unless, within 7 days from the date of this letter, we receive from you a replacement bank draft for £5,000, county court proceedings will be issued against you without further warning or notice.
>
> Yours faithfully,

To avoid being overlooked, it is recommended that the notice of dishonour be sent immediately the creditor becomes aware the cheque has been dishonoured.

4.4.2　Retention of title

A customer is in financial difficulties. He cannot make payments, and the creditor fears that, as the customer is about to go out of business, recovery through court action will be too late. Alternatively, the customer has already been declared insolvent. It is too late to obtain payment but, if the customer continues to hold goods, and there is a retention of title clause incorporated in the creditor's contract, return of those goods can be sought.

How is a retention of title clause enforced? First, can the goods be identified? If not, the claim will fail. This will also be the case where goods have been sold onwards, unless the sale proceeds can be identified. Also, if the goods have been incorporated so that they are no longer identifiable, such as resin incorporated in furniture, again, the claim will fail.

Assuming, however, these various tests can be satisfied, a creditor should notify its customers or the appointed receiver immediately of its claim and make arrangements for removal of the goods. The person having control of the goods should be put on notice that, if the goods are disposed of, an action for damages for conversion will be made against them personally. If access to inspect the goods or removal is refused, force should not be employed but consideration should be given to seeking an injunction to protect the creditor's position.

4.4.3 Recording sales negotiations

Companies should encourage their sales departments to make a record of meetings and telephone attendances. When a dispute arises, a contemporaneous note will carry greater weight than someone attempting to recall events at a distance in time. Where there are subsequent variations in a contract, these should be noted.

When a dispute arises, signed dated statements should be obtained from those employees who had dealings with the contract. There may be a need for future clarification once full details of the defence are disclosed, but an initial statement will assist the creditor in assessing the prospects for the claim.

4.4.4 Separate rights of action

The creditor may have obtained a guarantee or charge. Where the debtor defaults, demand should be made on this third party security and copies of the documents and correspondence provided.

4.4.5 Timing

Whatever the nature of the dispute, its timing will have a material bearing on its prospects for success. Certain defects may only become apparent sometime after the date of supply but, as a general rule, one would expect disputes to be raised immediately.

Therefore, a creditor should keep copies of correspondence and accounts chasing late payment or, where these are in standard form, have the ability to reproduce them. If it can be shown that a dispute is only raised subsequent to reminders for payment, the debtor will face an uphill struggle convincing the court that his is a valid defence.

4.5 Letters before action

4.5.1 Are they necessary?

It is usual, but not compulsory, for a letter before action to be sent before proceedings are commenced. A well-versed credit controller will have implemented a system of reminders by letter and telephone to suit his business once an invoice becomes overdue. Whilst the wording can be tailored to the needs of any given business, a suggested specimen letter follows:

> Dear Sirs,
>
> Account reference 5479
>
> We are concerned to note that despite reminders for payment your account in the sum of £5,000 remains owing. Accordingly, unless within 7 days from the date of this letter we receive from you your currently dated cheque in satisfaction proceedings for recovery will be issued and served without further warning or notice.
>
> Yours faithfully,

Once a creditor perceives that it is necessary to issue proceedings to recover payment, can a letter before action be dispensed with or should immediate proceedings follow? There may be overriding considerations which determine immediate issue, such as reliable indications within the trade that a creditor is in severe financial difficulty. However, these are the exceptions and, as a general rule, a letter before action is recommended.

Receipt of such a letter may produce immediate payment or cause many debtors to put forward proposals for a schedule of repayments. The short delay resulting from sending the letter is likely to be more than compensated for by the response rate.

There is another practical consideration. As will be seen, a successful creditor is entitled to look to the debtor for payment of statutory interest and the fixed costs of proceedings. Where payment of the principal debt is made after issue of the proceedings, the debtor may argue that he received no notification of intention to issue proceedings and, therefore, should not pay those costs and interest. If a suitably worded letter before action has been sent, that argument must fail.

Otherwise, the conduct of the debtor and the notification given to him will need to be examined. Was there, for instance, a failure to maintain a previously agreed schedule of repayments or a dishonoured cheque? Reminders may have been given by the creditor, but did these constitute sufficient notice to the debtor that proceedings would follow if payment was not made? Failure to give sufficient notice increases litigation cost. As a general rule, letters before action should always be sent.

4.5.2 What do they say?

Whatever the letter, to maximise its impact, pre-printed forms incorporating typed-in debt details should be avoided. The following should be included:

(1)   The full and correct name and address of the debtor. This may include the reference or be marked for the attention of a particular individual. Where the debtor has several addresses, the payment section should be used.
(2)   The date. A copy of the letter should be retained or another means of recalling the text should be employed.
(3)   The creditor's full title, including any trading name.
(4)   The amount owing. This will normally include invoices subject to dispute but omit invoices not yet due.
(5)   Requirement of payment within a specified period, usually seven days or less.
(6)   The address to which payment should be made. There should be a clear indication that failure to make payment as specified will result in the issue of proceedings. Even where there is an earlier breach in payment terms, only overdue invoices should be pursued by letter and action.

The letter should be clear and concise, avoiding waffle. The message should be unmistakable: pay or proceedings will follow.

4.5.3   What else can be included in the letter?

The cost of the letter will be borne by the creditor unless, unusually, the debtor can be persuaded to make payment. Interest for late payment will be recoverable only if that is incorporated as a term of the contract.

4.5.4   Should a letter before action be sent as a bluff?

As a general rule, never threaten a course of action unless prepared to follow it through. This applies as much with a letter before action as any other stage in the legal process.

If the letter states that proceedings will be taken after, say, seven days and there have been neither satisfactory proposals nor payment at the end of that period, then proceedings should be issued at that time. The debtor will then know that the creditor means business. A delay, of perhaps six weeks, gives out a signal to the debtor, rightly or wrongly, that the creditor is half-hearted in its pursuit of the action.

There may, however, be some debtors where it would be uneconomic to issue proceedings, and in those circumstances it may be worthwhile, as a last try, to send a letter before action but not pursue the matter further.

Chapter 5

WHICH COURT?

5.1   Jurisdiction

For the collection of debts in England and Wales, creditors must employ either the High Court or county court. The scope of this book is limited to county court actions only. Whilst the two court systems overlap, as a general rule the county court deals with lower value claims and the procedures adopted are slightly more informal. The majority of proceedings issued by parties acting in person are in the county court and a limited company taking or defending proceedings itself must use the county court unless it has its own in-house lawyer. There are about 270 county court offices throughout the country. Steps in court proceedings can be dealt with either by post or over the counter of the court office. Details of standard forms and fees can be obtained from the court staff. Forms can be obtained from the court itself or from law stationers.

- Scotland, Northern Ireland, the Isle of Man, and individual Channel Islands have their own legal systems.

- Proceedings can be issued in the county court against foreign companies having trading addresses in England and Wales.

- Similar proceedings to those outlined here for the recovery of debts are available in actions for damages for breach of contract.

- Injunctions can prove a speedy but expensive remedy to prevent a debtor from taking action, eg disposal of assets, which may be prejudicial to a creditor's interests.

- Consider instructing solicitors experienced in collection work if an action becomes too complex.

5.2   County court

It is for the creditor to determine in which county court he will commence proceedings. For convenience this is likely to be the nearest county court to him but may as readily be the debtor's home court. County courts are usually listed in the telephone directory under 'Courts'. If a defence to an action is filed, proceedings will be transferred automatically to the debtor's home county court. Equally, once execution has been issued any enforcement action, even where the warrant has been issued in another county court, will be taken by the bailiff for the debtor's home court.

For the benefit of bulk users, the courts have introduced the Summons Production Centre in Northampton. This arranges for issue of proceedings throughout the country. It is fast and efficient, having the added advantage of cheaper fees on issue of proceedings than those forwarded to the individual courts for issue. The Summons Production Centre is able to prepare and issue summonses from computer-readable information.

Creditors may have come across the expression 'The Small Claims Court'. There is no separate small claims court. Small claims are dealt with in the county court. As a general rule, when disputed, small claims, currently under £3,000, are referred to arbitration rather than trial. This will be covered in more detail later.

The words employed by the courts can be off-putting for those unfamiliar with legal proceedings. There is no great mystery to the terminology, however. The party taking the proceedings is known as the Plaintiff. The party against whom the proceedings are brought is the Defendant. In an undisputed action, neither party is likely to have any dealings with the judiciary. Most of the routine applications covered in this text will be heard by district judges. Only more complex matters and trials are dealt with by the more senior county court judges.

The court's 'Bible' for rules and procedure is *The County Court Practice*, invariably known as the Green Book. This is updated annually. Weighing in at more than 2,000 pages, its price and complexity make it too daunting an investment for anyone other than a practising lawyer. A creditor should be aware of its existence, however, as it may be referred to should disputes arise in proceedings.

Chapter 6

STARTING PROCEEDINGS

6.1 The procedure

Claims for recovery of debts are begun by default summons (Form N1). This is prepared by the Plaintiff. The Summons sets out the court details, the names and addresses of the parties, together with the amount and nature of the claim. If the particulars of the claim are lengthy, these should be shown on a separate sheet, headed Particulars of Claim. The Plaintiff should forward to the court three copies of the Summons, the fee payable by cheque in favour of 'HMPG Lord Chancellor's Department', and three copies of any separate Particulars of Claim. The court will retain one set of copies for their own use, serve the second set on the Defendant and return the third set to the Plaintiff. Where there is more than one Defendant, the Plaintiff will need to lodge one extra copy of the Summons and Particulars of Claim for each additional Defendant.

The Summons is issued by the court who arrange for service, confirming to the Plaintiff. The next step will be determined by the Defendant's response.

6.2 Completing the Summons

Every straightforward debt action is commenced by a form of default summons, Form N1. This is completed by the Plaintiff. An example of a completed Court Summons is shown at the end of this chapter. How kindly the Defendant took to these proceedings is not a matter of record.

6.2.1 Interest

The Plaintiff can claim either contractual or statutory interest. Contractual interest only applies where it is agreed between the parties, at or subsequent to the contract, that the buyer will pay interest at a specified rate to the seller in the event of late payment.

Entitlement to contractual interest can be difficult to prove, especially if it has been agreed in a conversation. Far more common is a claim for statutory interest at the rate set by the Lord Chancellor's department, currently 8% per annum. In either case, interest will be calculated on the sum being claimed from the invoice due date to the date on which the Summons is being prepared. The due date will vary from claim to claim, depending on the terms of the contract. An invoice might, for instance, be payable immediately or after 30 days. Where several invoices due on different dates are involved, a series of calculations will be required to reach the interest total. Interest in county court actions can be claimed to the entry of judgment. For claims exceeding £5,000, interest subsequent to judgment may be claimable.

6.3   Particulars of Claim

Whether the Particulars of Claim can be contained on the form of Summons or appear on a different sheet is essentially a question of the amount of information to be included. It should usually be possible to contain all the relevant details of the claim in the space provided on the Summons, as shown in the above example. There is a risk, however, that if a claim is too vague or incomplete it is more likely to attract a defence or a request for further and better particulars of the Particulars of Claim, either of which will delay the action and increase its cost. Use the third person, ie 'The Plaintiff claims from the Defendant' rather than 'Associates owe me'. Certain information should and should not be included, however, depending upon whether the short or separate form is employed.

6.3.1   What to include

All the relevant facts should be included:

- The consideration forming the basis of the claim, eg goods sold and delivered.
- The debt being claimed – if there are a small number of invoices, a Plaintiff may prefer to list these separately. Whether they are listed individually or collectively, a global figure should always be shown.
- The invoice date(s) – where there are a large number of invoice dates refer to a period of supply between the first and last date.
- The invoice due date(s) – of importance for calculating interest.
- The basis on which interest is claimed – usually statutory entitlement.
- Interest owing to date.
- Daily rate at which interest accrues.
- Any admission of the debt.
- Any separate right of action – eg a dishonoured cheque.
- Identify any contractual documents relied upon – eg terms and conditions of trading.

6.3.2   What to exclude

- Anything that is not relevant to the claim before the court.
- Evidence – this is not the place for explaining who said what to whom on a particular date.

Above all, the Particulars of Claim should be clear and concise. There is no requirement that they should be printed or typed, but good presentation will help get the court on the Plaintiff's side.

A form of summons may, however, afford insufficient space for the particulars of a more complex claim. In that case, insert the appropriate type of claim (see example on Form N1 at the end of this chapter: 'ADVERTISING SERVICES') on the form and in the section for particulars of the claim 'as more particularly set out on the attached Particulars of Claim'. The remainder of the form of summons should be completed appropriately. The Particulars of Claim should appear on a separate sheet, including the heading of the action, as set out in the following example.

IN THE BRISTOL COUNTY COURT   Case Number

BETWEEN

A. N. BODY t/a Work Services   Plaintiff

and

ANY COMPANY LIMITED   Defendant

PARTICULARS OF CLAIM

1. The Plaintiff is in the business of hiring out labour and machinery.
2. On or about 15 May 1995 by agreement PN127 the Plaintiff hired to the Defendant at its site in Main Street, Bristol, a compressor and operative at the rate of £50 per day and £12 per hour respectively. The set period of hire was for fourteen days from 15–29 May 1995.
3. On or about 29 May 1995 by agreement PN138 the Plaintiff hired to the Defendant at its site in Back Street, Bristol, a compressor at the rate of £50 per day. The set period of hire was for seven days from 30 May–5 June 1995.
4. Pursuant to the said agreements there is owing by the Defendant

Invoice	Date	Due Date	Amount
IN127	30.05.95	30.06.95	£1,660
IN138	6.06.95	31.07.95	£ 350
			£2,010
Less Deposit			£ 250
			£1,760

5. By letter dated 13.6.95 the Defendants offered to make repayments at the rate of £200 per week which the Plaintiff accepted by its letter dated 14.6.95.
6. No payment has been received by the Plaintiff and the Defendant remains indebted in the sum of £1,760.
7. Further, the Plaintiff claims interest thereon pursuant to Section 69 of the County Courts Act 1984 at the rate of 8% per annum from the invoice due dates to the date hereof and continuing until judgment or earlier payment. Interest to date totals £20.82 and continues to accrue at the daily rate of £0.46.

AND The Plaintiff claims the sum of £1,760 together with £20.82 interest and further interest accruing at £0.46 per day until judgment or earlier payment.

DATED 21 August 1995

                                        A. N. Body
                                        ....
                                        The Plaintiff

TO The Court

AND TO The Defendant

An edited version of the claim could be incorporated into the form of summons, however, the additional information regarding the substance of the claim and the Defendant's letter of admission make any attempt at a defence that much more difficult to sustain.

In earlier chapters, reference has been made to the importance of having up-to-date trading terms and conditions and ensuring that these are incorporated in the contract. The importance of sending notice of dishonour when a cheque fails to be met has also been discussed. Both these points are covered in the following example.

IN THE SOUTHPORT COUNTY COURT   Case No

BETWEEN

SUPPLIERS LTD t/a Clothes   Plaintiff

and

T. BROWN (male) and T. JONES (female) T/A Bad Payers   Defendants

PARTICULARS OF CLAIM

1. During December 1995 the Plaintiff supplied to the Defendants at their request children's clothes.

Particulars

Invoice	Date	Due Date	Amount
PG12	1.12.95	31.12.95	£540
PG41	12.12.95	11.01.95	£320
			£860

2. It was an express term of the contract between the parties that any complaint regarding the quality of the goods delivered must be made by the Defendants to the Plaintiff in writing within 7 days from delivery.
3. No complaint regarding the quality of the said garments has been made within the specified period or at all.
4. On 12 December 1995, the Defendants provided to the Plaintiff's agent a cheque for £540 in settlement of invoice PG12. The said cheque dated 12 December 1995 was drawn on the Defendant's account number 123456 at Lloyd's Bank, Highgate Branch. The cheque was returned 'Refer to Drawer' and on 14 December 1995 the Plaintiff sent notice of dishonour to the Defendant.
5. Further, the Plaintiff claims interest on the said £860 pursuant to Section 69 of the County Courts Act 1984 as amended at the rate of 8% per annum from the invoice due date to the date hereof in the sum of £1.46 and continuing until judgment or earlier payment at the daily rate of £0.11.

AND The Plaintiff claims the sum of £860 together with £1.46 interest and further interest of £0.11 per day until judgment or earlier payment.

DATED 12 January 1996

M. Polo

....

A duly authorised officer of the Plaintiff

TO The Court

AND TO The Defendants

The extra information at paragraphs 2 and 3 above makes it difficult for the Defendants to mount a successful defence claiming the garments were sub-standard. The inclusion of the notice of dishonour (paragraph 4) makes it impossible for the Defendants to mount a sustainable defence as to £540 in any event.

6.4   Service of proceedings

Service of the Summons and any separate Particulars of Claim is effected by first-class post and is arranged by the court. The proceedings are deemed to be served two days after posting on a Defendant limited company at its registered office, seven days after posting on any other Defendant. Form N225, Notice of Issue of Default Summons, is returned by the court to the Plaintiff endorsed with the date of postal service. All future court documents prepared by the Plaintiff should include the full heading in the action including details of parties, the court and case number. The Plaintiff will be in a position to make application for judgment 14 days from the date of postal service.

The vast majority of Summonses issued are served by post, but difficulties with postal service may be encountered. A Plaintiff faced with an evasive Defendant may opt for service by the court bailiff either in the first instance or after attempting postal service. The request is by letter to the court. There is a small additional service fee of £10 payable and a consequential increase in the amount of fixed costs recoverable from the Defendant.

The bailiff will only attempt to effect service at the address provided. Where a Defendant has moved or furnished a false address it is for the Plaintiff to establish the Defendant's current whereabouts. If the Plaintiff's own enquiries are not successful he may consider instructing enquiry agents in an attempt to trace the Defendant and can employ them to serve the Summons. The Plaintiff should bear in mind that the Summons is only valid for four months. If problems regarding service are being experienced, application to renew the Summons should be made before the four-month period expires.

The Defendant has 14 days from service in which to take action.

- No action by the Defendant – immediate application for judgment should be made (Form N30), together with application for enforcement of the judgment.
- Payment in full is made by the Defendant – no action,
- Defendant is bankrupt or wound-up – no further action in proceedings.
- Defendant enters defence – contested proceedings, consider possibility of summary judgment application.
- Defendant serves defence and counterclaim – Plaintiff has 14 days in which to serve defence to counterclaim.
- Defendant enters admission – no separate application for judgment is required. Proceed to enforce.
- Defendant enters admission, offering to pay by instalments – either the Plaintiff completes Form N225, accepting the offer, the court enters

judgment and the Defendant makes payment to the Plaintiff, or the Plaintiff completes Form N225, rejecting the offer and setting out grounds.

- An authorised court officer determines the level of repayments and enters judgment. If either party objects to the repayments ordered, it may apply for a disposal hearing to review the level of repayments.
- The Defendant admits only part of the claim – enter judgment for admitted sum. Disputed balance is a contested action – consider summary judgment option.

Flowchart: Initiating proceedings

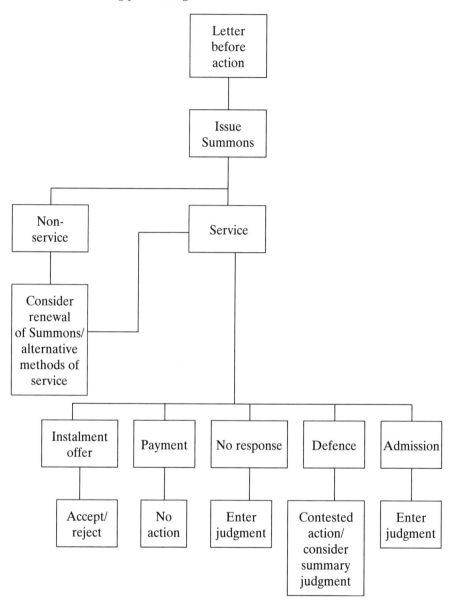

County Court Summons

Case Number	*Always quote this*	

In the ①

TOMBSTONE

County Court

The court office is open from 10am to 4pm Monday to Friday

Telephone:

Seal

This summons is only valid if sealed by the court
If it is not sealed it should be reported to the court
Keep this summons. You may need to refer to it

(1) Plaintiff's full name address

TOMBSTONE GAZETTE LTD, ②
SUNDANCE BUILDING, ③
HIGH NOON STREET,
TOMBSTONE

(2) Address for sending documents and payments *(if not as above)*
Ref/Tel no.

— ④

(3) Defendant's full name *(eg Mr, Mrs or Miss where known)*
and address Company no. *(where known)*

WYATT EARP, ⑤
THE GOLDEN NUGGET SALOON,
LITTLE BIG MAN ROAD,
BLACK GULTCH

What the plaintiff claims from you

Brief description of type of claim

ADVERTISING SERVICES ⑥

⑦ Particulars of the plaintiff's claim against you

THE PLAINTIFF'S CLAIM IS THE SUM OF £158·70 IN RESPECT OF THE PRICE OF ADVERTISING SERVICES PROVIDED TO THE DEFENDANT'S ORDER, TOGETHER WITH INTEREST PURSUANT TO SECTION 69 OF THE COUNTY COURTS ACT 1984 AS AMENDED AT THE RATE OF 8% PER ANNUM FROM THE DATE PAYMENT FELL DUE (BEING 30 DAYS FROM THE DATE OF EACH RESPECTIVE INVOICE) TO THE DATE HEREOF AND CONTINUING UNTIL JUDGMENT OR EARLIER PAYMENT. INTEREST TO DATE AMOUNTS TO £1·95 AND CONTINUES AT A DAILY RATE OF £0·03.

INVOICE	DATE	AMOUNT
AB 34	1·10·95	£215·00
AB 45	28·10·95	138·15
		353·15
LESS PAID	13·11·95	194·45
		£158·70

⑫

Signed   *Tombstone Gazette Ltd*
Plaintiff or plaintiff's solicitor
(or see enclosed particulars of claim)

JN1 Default summons (fixed amount) (Order 3, rule 3(2)(b)) (1.96)

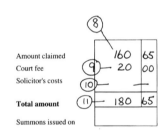

		⑧	
Amount claimed		160	65
Court fee	⑨	20	00
Solicitor's costs	⑩	—	
Total amount	⑪	180	65
Summons issued on			

What to do about this summons

You have 21 days from the date of the postmark to reply to this summons
(A limited company served at its registered office has 16 days to reply)
If this summons was delivered by hand, you have 14 days from the date it was delivered to reply

You can

- dispute the claim
- make a claim against the plaintiff
- admit the claim and costs in full and offer to pay
- admit only part of the claim
- pay the total amount shown above

You must read the information on the back of this form. It will tell you more about what to do.

1 The name of the court.
2 The Plaintiff's full name – an individual should be shown as 'Francis Brown' not 'F. Brown'. Unless there is insufficient space, all partners and the firm's name should be referred to. 'Francis Brown, Thomas Smith and Andrew Jones T/A Associates', rather than 'Associates'. Where the Plaintiff is a Limited Company, the name of the company, rather than that of any individuals, should be shown.
3 The Plaintiff's full address – do not use PO Box numbers. Where there is more than one trading address for a firm, use the main office. If the Plaintiff is a Limited Company its Registered Office should be shown, and identified as such by writing 'R/O' beside it.
4 Address for service and payment (if different from the Plaintiff's address). This additional information will be required only from larger organisations or, particularly, where a limited company's registered office differs from its trading address. Consider which address and reference to insert. A payments section may be quite competent to deal with monthly instalments from the Defendant but would they know how to respond to a defence and counterclaim?
5 The Defendant's name and address – the comments regarding the Plaintiff's name and address apply equally and are of even greater significance. Do check information is full and accurate. The wrong name will mean wasted time and costs. An incomplete name may hinder execution. If judgment is obtained in the name of a firm only, it can only be enforced against the assets of the firm. A separate application, entailing cost and delay, would be required to proceed against the proprietor's assets. Better to identify both the firm name and the partners so that immediate execution can follow on both fronts.

A PO Box should be sufficient for service of the Summons, but a postal address will be required if subsequent enforcement action is needed. For a limited company, either its registered office or a place of business of the company having connection with the subject matter of the proceedings should be used.

Where the debtor has instructed solicitors and they have confirmed they will accept service of proceedings, their name and address should be added as the address for service.
6 Brief description of the claim – typically this might be 'goods sold and delivered', 'haulage services', 'storage charges', 'advertising' or 'professional services'. There are any number of variations depending on the nature of the Plaintiff's business.
7 Particulars of the claim – these will comprise either details of the claim, or, where these are lengthier, and appear on a separate Particulars of Claim, an endorsement 'shown on Particulars of Claim'. See **6.3**.
8 The amount claimed – this is a global figure. If several sums are being claimed from the Defendant these should be added to any interest and shown as a single figure. (With regard to interest, see **6.2.1**).
9 The court fee – the following scale of fees applies:

Claims not exceeding	Fee
£100	£10
£200	£20
£300	£30
£400	£40
£500	£50
£600	£60
£1,000	£65
£5,000	£70
£ unlimited	£80

Where proceedings are issued out of the Summons Production Centre, discounted fees apply. Bear in mind that a party acting in person who is in receipt of income support is exempt from payment of standard court fees.
10 Solicitor's costs – a Plaintiff acting on its own behalf who is not a solicitor should ignore this section. The exception to this is where a plaintiff company or Body Corporate has its own in-house legal department, including solicitors, who have conduct of the action.
11 Total amount – the amount claimed plus court fee and solicitor's costs, if appropriate.
12 Signature – remember to sign the form.

jORDANS © Crown Copyright

Request for Judgment and reply to Admission

(default action - fixed amount)

- *Tick and complete either A or B. Make sure that all the case details are given and that the judgment details at C are completed. Remember to sign and date the form. Your signature certifies that the information you have given is correct.*

- *If the defendant has given and address on the form of admission to which correspondence should be sent, which is different from the address shown on the summons, you will need to tell the court*

In the	STRATFORD - UPON - AVON
	County Court
Case Number Always quote this	965001
Plaintiff	WILLIAM SHAKESPEARE
Defendant	CHRISTOPHER MARLOW PLAYS LTD.
Plaintiff's Ref.	

A ☐ **The defendant has not replied to my summons**

Complete all the judgment details at C. Decide how and when you want the defendant to pay. You can ask for the judgement to be paid by instalments or in one payment.

B ☐ **The defendant admits that all the money is owed**

Tick only one box below and return the completed slip to the court.

☐ **I accept the defendant's proposal for payment**

Complete all the judgment details at C. Say how the defendant intends to pay. The court will send the defendant an order to pay. You will also be sent a copy.

☐ **The defendant has not made any proposal for payment**

Complete all the judgment details at C. Say how you want the defendant to pay. You can ask for the judgment to be paid by instalments or in one payment. The court will send the defendant an order to pay. You will also be sent a copy.

☐ **I do NOT accept the defendant's proposal for payment**

Complete all the judgment details at C and say how you want the defendant to pay. Give your reasons for objecting to the defendant's offer of payment in the space opposite. (Continue on the back of this form if necessary.) Send this form to the court **together with the defendant's admission N9A** (or a copy). The court will fix a rate of payment and send the defendant an order to pay. You will also be sent a copy.

C Judgment details

I would like the judgment to be paid

☑ (forthwith) *only tick this box if you intend to enforce the order right away*

☐ (by instalments of £ _____ per month)

☐ (in full by _____)

Amount of claim as stated in summons (including interest at date of issue)......................	1415	38
Interest since date of summons (if any)................	4	96
Period 16 Rate 8 %		
Court fees shown on summons	70	00
Solicitor's costs (if any) on issuing summons		
Sub Total	1490	34
Solicitor's costs (if any) on entering judgment	—	
Sub Total	1490	34
Deduct amount (if any) paid since issue	250	00
Amount payable by defendant	1240	34

I certify that the information given is correct

| Signed | *W Shakespeare* | Plaintiff ('s ~~solicitor~~) | **Dated** | 30/6/96 |

N225 (Request for judgment and reply to admission in default action (fixed amount) (Order 9, rule 3)   Reproduced with the permission of the Controller of Her Majesty's Stationery Office   JN225 6/91

Chapter 7

JUDGMENT BY DEFAULT OR ADMISSION

Provided that no problems over service are experienced, the Plaintiff may find itself facing six possible scenarios. They are as follows:

- the Defendant takes no action;
- the Defendant admits debt/part debt;
- the Defendant admits debt/part debt and offers to pay by instalments;
- the Defendant pays;
- the Defendant is insolvent;
- the Defendant defends the action.

The final scenario, a defended action, is considered in the next chapter. The remainder are dealt with below.

7.1 The defendant takes no action

As discussed in the previous chapter, the Defendant has 14 days from the date of postal service in which to lodge its defence with the court. Immediately after 14 days the Plaintiff should apply for judgment to protect its position. This can either be a separate request for judgment (see Form N225 at end of chapter 6), or the request attached to the Notice of Issue of Default Summons. The wording is identical in either case. Plaintiffs should ensure that they tick all relevant boxes and that the form is signed and dated, otherwise it will be returned by the court. Most of the information to be inserted can be taken direct from the Summons. A simple calculation of further interest will need to be inserted. A party acting in person will not be entitled to solicitor's costs. There is no fee payable.

A copy should be retained for the Plaintiff's file and the original forwarded to the court with a covering letter. If a defence has been lodged with the court, the application will be returned. Provided there is no defence, judgment will be recorded by the court. An unsatisfied judgment is registered and is liable to affect the Defendant's credit rating.

Judgment does not, however, guarantee payment. Creditors often mistakenly think that obtaining judgment is the end of the battle. This is far from the truth, but judgment is an important step in the proceedings, providing confirmation by the court that the sum claimed is properly owing. Once judgment is obtained, steps to enforce that judgment should be taken, see Chapter 10. To save time it is sensible to send with the request for judgment an application to enforce.

7.2   The defendant admits debt/part debt

Often the Defendant admits the debt either by completing the pre-printed form provided to it by the court or in separate correspondence. In such circumstances the Plaintiff should make application for judgment as set out above, ticking Box B on Form N205A and the appropriate box below this. If the letter admitting the debt has not previously been seen by the court a copy should be provided with the application.

The Defendant may admit part of the debt but dispute the remainder. The Plaintiff should enter judgment for the admitted sum, treating the balance as a defended action (see Chapter 8).

7.3   The defendant admits debt/part debt and offers to pay by instalments

In such cases, the part of the debt which is not admitted is treated as a defended action. The admitted part is dealt with as set out in **7.2** but, in addition, the Plaintiff must determine whether or not to accept the Defendant's offer which may be either for monthly payments or payment in full within a specified time.

An example of a Form of Admission, complete with financial particulars and offer of payment is attached. The Plaintiff should complete Form N205A as set out earlier.

7.3.1   Accept offer

If the offer is acceptable or appears to the Plaintiff to be all that the Defendant can afford, the Plaintiff should tick the boxes at B confirming that the Defendant admits the money is owed and that the Plaintiff accepts the proposed method of repayment. The Plaintiff should also complete the appropriate section for the judgment details indicating the amount of monthly payments or when full payment is due.

7.3.2   Reject offer

If the Defendant's offer is rejected, the Plaintiff should tick the box indicating this and complete judgment details in the normal way, usually requiring payment forthwith. The Plaintiff should provide written reasons for rejecting the offer. This may be, for example, that on the figures the Defendant can afford higher payments or that the Defendant has failed to give accurate or complete information regarding his financial position. The completed form is returned to the court together with the Defendant's Form of Admission. The court then determines whether immediate payment should be made or, if not, what it considers an appropriate level of repayment. If the Plaintiff considers the court order does not reflect the Defendant's ability to pay it should write to the court indicating its objection to the terms of the order and requesting a disposal hearing. At that hearing, both parties will have the opportunity to attend before the district judge and make representations regarding what they consider an appropriate level for the repayment of the debt. The district judge may alter or ratify the earlier order.

Whether agreeing to or, more particularly, opposing the Defendant's offer the Plaintiff should ensure that it responds to the court within 14 days. Otherwise, the court will make such order as it sees fit.

7.4 The defendant pays

If the Defendant pays in full, no further action is required from the Plaintiff. If part of the debt, interest or the Summons fee remains outstanding, the Plaintiff should enter judgment for that balance.

7.5 The defendant is insolvent

The Defendant may claim, in its admission to the court or in direct communication with the Plaintiff, that it has no assets and no ability to pay. It is a commercial decision for the Plaintiff whether to accept such a statement at face value, instigate further enquiries or carry on with the proceedings in any event. The obvious risk is that the Plaintiff may be throwing good money after bad.

7.5.1 Companies

The Defendant may be formally insolvent. The following are the most common examples:

- The Defendant company is in receivership – the Plaintiff can continue with its action but this is likely to be a waste of money as all company assets will be claimed by the receiver.
- The Defendant company is in liquidation – no further steps in the proceedings can be taken without leave of the court.

7.5.2 Individuals

Where the Plaintiff is pursuing an individual Defendant, the Defendant may be declared bankrupt. In such circumstances all assets vest in the Trustee in Bankruptcy.

Alternatively, a Defendant may make application for an Individual Voluntary Arrangement (IVA). This is a form of agreement between the debtor and his creditors to repay them in full or in part over a period of time. An insolvency practitioner must first put a proposal to the court. If successful, an Interim Order will be made. This prevents, for a period of time, any steps from being taken in proceedings by creditors who are advised of the Interim Order. A meeting of creditors is convened where the creditors vote to reject, vary or agree the IVA. If the proposal is rejected, proceedings can continue when the

Interim Order expires. If the IVA is ratified, all notified creditors are bound by it.

7.5.3   Action by creditor

What then should a Plaintiff do when faced with a Defendant who is insolvent? If suppliers, by their terms and conditions have retained ownership of the goods supplied pending payment, they should immediately pursue their claims against those goods held by the Defendant, if they have not already done so. Otherwise, the creditors will have to wait for the liquidator or Trustee in Bankruptcy to distribute amongst them any surplus assets after payment of the secured and preferential creditors. Secured creditors would most commonly be mortgagees of property owned by the Defendant. Preferential creditors include, for example, the Inland Revenue. Realistically, the prospects for trade creditors receiving anything more than a small dividend as unsecured creditors in a bankruptcy or liquidation are slight. Claims should be notified to the Trustee or liquidator. Depending on the size of the debt and any suspicious circumstances, the Plaintiff should elect whether or not it is worthwhile attending personally at the meeting of creditors, or to be represented by a solicitor or an accountant.

Form for Replying to a Summons

- *Read the notes on the summons before completing this form*
- *Tick the correct boxes and give the other details asked for*
- *Send or take this completed and signed form immediately to the court office shown on the summons*
- *You should keep your copy of the summons*
- **For details of where and how to pay see the summons**

What is your full name? (BLOCK CAPITALS)

Surname CAESAR

Forenames JULIUS

Mr ☑ Mrs ☐ Miss ☐ Ms ☐

How much of the claim do you admit?

☐ **All of it** (complete only sections 1 and 2)

☑ **Part of it** (sections 1,2,3,4,5) **Amount** £ 750 : OO

☐ **None of it** (complete sections 3,4 and 5 overleaf)

Section 1   Offer of payment

I offer to pay the amount admitted on (date) 25/10/96
or for the reasons set out below

I cannot pay the amount admitted in one instalment

but I can pay by monthly instalments of   £ 100 : OO

Fill in the next section as fully as possible. Your answers will help the plaintiff decide whether your offer is realistic and ought to be accepted. Your answers will also help the court, if necessary, to fix a rate of payment that you can afford.

Section 2   Income and outgoings

a. Employment I am

☐ Unemployed

☐ A pensioner

☐ Self employed as

☑ Employed as a   TRIBUNE

My employer is PAX ROMANICA LTD

Employer's address: THE FORUM
                      MILTON KEYNES

b. Income *specify period: weekly, fortnightly, monthly etc.*

My usual take home pay   £ 750 : per month

Child benefit(s) total   £   :

Other state benefit(s) total   £   :

My pension(s) total   £   :

Other people living in my
home give me   £   :

Other income (give details)   £   :

In the STRATFORD-UPON-AVON
                                    County Court

Case Number *Always quote this* 965002

Plaintiff *(including reference)*
          BRUTUS LTD

Defendant
          JULIUS CAESAR

c. Bank account and savings

☐ I do not have a bank account

☑ I have a bank account

The account is ☐ in credit ☑ overdrawn by £ 70 : 00

☐ I do not have a savings account

☑ I have a savings account

The amount in the account is   £ 250 : 00

d. Dependants *(people you look after financially)*

Number of dependants FOUR
(give ages of children) 12, 10, 7

e. Outgoings

I make regular payments as follows:

	weekly	monthly		
Mortgage	☐	☑	£	250 : 00
Rent	☐	☐	£	:
Mail order	☐	☑	£	50 : 00
TV rental/licence	☐	☐	£	:
HP repayments	☐	☑	£	25 : 00
Court orders	☐	☑	£	25 : 00

specify period: yearly, quarterly, etc.

Gas	£	50 : 00
Electricity	£	25 : 00
Council tax	£	30 : 00
Water charges	£	20 : 00
Other regular payments (give details below)		MONTHLY

£   :

Credit card and other debts *(please list)*

£   :

Of the payments above, I am behind with payments to

£   :

---

continue on a separate sheet if necessary – put the case number in the top right hand corner

Give an address to which notices about this case should be sent to you

6 CATULLUS CLOSE
NEWPORT PAGNALL
                  Postcode 6ET 7U8

I declare that the details I have given above are true to the best of my knowledge

Signed *(to be signed by you or by your solicitor)* J. Caesar

Position *(if signing on behalf of firm or company)*

Dated 25/9/96

N9 Form of admission, defence and counterclaim to accompany Forms N2, 3 and 4 (Order 3, rule 3(2)(c))   11.95

Case No. ....

Section 3 Defending the claim: defence	Section 4 Making a claim against the plaintiff: counterclaim

Fill in this part of the form only if you wish to defend the claim or part of the claim.

a.   How much of the plaintiff's claim do you dispute?

All of it ☐

Part of it ☑   *give amount*   £ 350:00

If you dispute only part of the claim, you must complete sections 1 and 2 overleaf and part b. below.

b.   What are your reasons for disputing the claim?

METAL PRODUCTS PROVIDED BY
PLAINTIFF NOT OF MERCHANTABLE
QUALITY

Fill in this part of the form only if you wish to make a claim against the plaintiff.
If your claim against the plaintiff is for more than his claim against you, you may have to pay a fee. Ask at the court office whether a fee is payable.

a.   What is the nature of the claim you wish to make against the plaintiff?

b.   If your claim is for a specific sum of money, how much are you claiming?

£ ....

c.   What are your reasons for making the claim?

continue on a separate sheet if necessary – put the case number in the top right hand corner

Section 5 Arbitration under the small claims procedure

How the claim will be dealt with if defended

If the total the plaintiff is claiming is £3,000 or less, it will be dealt with by arbitration (small claims procedure) unless the court decides the case is too difficult to be dealt with in this informal way. Costs and the grounds for setting aside an arbitration award are strictly limited. If the claim is not dealt with by arbitration, costs, including the costs of help from a legal representative, may be allowed.

If the total the plaintiff is claiming is more than £3,000, it can still be dealt with by arbitration if you or the plaintiff ask for it and the court approves. If your claim is dealt with by arbitration in these circumstances, costs may be allowed.

Please tick this box if you would like the claim dealt with by arbitration ☐

Give an address to which notices about this case should be sent to you	Signed *(to be signed by you or by your solicitor)*
6 CATALLUS CLOSE NEWPORT PAGNELL	*J. Caesar*
Postcode MET TU8 Dated	Position *(if signing on behalf of firm or company)* 25/9/96

Chapter 8

DEFENDED ACTIONS

In this chapter, outline consideration is given on how to deal with defended actions, the standard procedures leading to the trial of the claim, whether summary judgment is appropriate and the procedures to be followed if a Plaintiff does not want to pursue an action to trial.

8.1 Defence filed

Once a Defence is filed, if the action was commenced elsewhere than in the Defendant's home county court the proceedings will be transferred to that court. The Defence may be on the standard form provided by the court or on a separate sheet. The Defence may only relate to part of the claim, in which case the Plaintiff is entitled to proceed to judgment for the undisputed balance. The Defendant may be acting on its own behalf or have instructed a solicitor. A Plaintiff acting on its own behalf must determine whether it wishes to continue to do so, whether it should also instruct a solicitor or whether it would prefer to seek a compromise of the action.

8.1.1 Pleadings

The Plaintiff may not be clear regarding certain allegations made in the Defence. The Plaintiff is entitled to request Further and Better Particulars of the Defence in writing provided the matter is proceeding to trial rather than arbitration (see **8.2**). If the Defendant fails to provide these, the Plaintiff may issue a Summons and obtain an order for the information on a hearing before the court. Where a defence is inaccurate or misleading, the Plaintiff may want to file with the court and serve on the Defendant a reply setting out the correct factual position. The defence may include a counter-claim, eg that money is owing by the Plaintiff to the Defendant. The Plaintiff must serve a defence to a counter-claim. It has 14 days to do so, or longer if the Defendant consents. If a Plaintiff fails to prepare a defence, judgment may be entered against it on the counter-claim.

8.1.2 Common defences

Defences encountered may take many forms but among the most common are:

- 'I never contracted with the Plaintiff'. If a creditor has correctly identified its debtor, such an argument should be defeated.
- 'I never received the goods'. A signed proof of delivery will counter this defence. Creditors should be wary of unsigned proofs or a scrawled signature. The carrier or representative should insist on a clear signature

from a person in authority. Where a customer is collecting goods, a signed receipt should be required.

- 'That is not what we agreed'. It should be verified that the contract was for the goods/services agreed. Clear details on estimates, orders, correspondence and invoices can defeat a spurious defence. If the contract was by sample and the creditor has retained, for instance, proofs or artwork or fabric samples approved by its customer, these will strengthen the case.
- 'The goods are defective'. The nature of the dispute should be considered carefully. A sight of the goods should be required. They are themselves evidence in the proceedings. If this is a try-on or the goods have been tampered with, can the Plaintiff prove this? It may be necessary, although costly, to appoint an independent expert to determine the validity of such claims.
- 'I rejected the goods'. It must be for the Defendant to provide evidence of valid rejection of the goods and its right to do so.
- 'I want to return the goods'. Not wanting to or not being able to pay presents no defence, unless goods were supplied on a sale or return basis. A Plaintiff should weigh up, however, the Defendant's ability to pay and its own ability to re-sell. In certain circumstances, it may make economic sense to accept return of the goods provided that the Defendant is responsible for carriage charges.
- 'The goods arrived too late'. The Plaintiff should examine the contract terms. Is time of the essence? If so, were deadlines complied with? The contract documents and proof of delivery will be crucial here.
- 'I have a claim to off-set against the Plaintiff'. The Defendant may be doing work for the Plaintiff. In that case, he can set off a valid claim against money owing to him.
- 'I lost money because the Plaintiff failed to perform the contract'. A defence need not be restricted to a denial of liability. The Defendant can look to the Plaintiff for consequential loss he has suffered through any alleged breach of contract. Such counter-claims may include additional expense, loss of profits and penalties incurred. Again, it is for the Defendant to satisfy the court that he has a valid counter-claim. Was the Plaintiff aware, or could it reasonably have foreseen the loss his customer would suffer?

8.2   Trial or arbitration?

The final hearing to determine a defended action will either be by trial or arbitration. With a few exceptions, all claims not exceeding £3,000 are referred to arbitration. Unusually, a party may apply for an action referred to arbitration to be transferred for trial if, say, important or complex legal issues are involved. Usually, claims over £3,000 will be dealt with by trial.

Since the procedures involved leading up to the trial or arbitration differ, these are dealt with here separately. The more informal arbitration procedure is far better suited to a party acting in person. For claims over £3,000, it is suggested therefore that the Plaintiff represent to the court on issue or when the defence is received that if the action is defended the case should be referred to arbitration. Practice may vary from court to court and the Plaintiff should check with its local court office. The Defendant can also request arbitration on such claims when completing Form N9. The final decision whether to refer to arbitration rests with the court, who may also choose to refer a matter for arbitration without application by either party.

8.3   Procedure to trial

If the matter is not appropriate for arbitration when a defence is filed, the court will send both parties Notice of Automatic Directions (see Form N450 at end of this chapter). This sets out the timetable for bringing the action to trial. The timetable begins 14 days after service of the defence or 28 days if a counter-claim was served with the defence. The steps to be taken may be summarised as follows:

Period after close of pleadings	*Action required*
1. 28 days	Serve List of Documents.
2. 35 days	Inspection of documents.
3. 70 days	Disclosure of witness statement.
4. 6 months	Request hearing.
5. 15 months	Action automatically struck out if no request for hearing date.

Period before hearing	*Action required*
6. 14 days	Defendant advises Plaintiff of documents it wants in court bundle.
7. 7 days	Plaintiff to file bundle of documents etc.

These various steps are set out on the Notice of Automatic Directions. With the consent of the Defendant, 1, 2, and 4 can be varied to allow further time. The aim of the directions is twofold, first, to ensure open litigation where each party knows in advance of the trial its opponent's case and, secondly, so that at the trial the matter can be dealt with most efficiently and without delay.

8.3.1   The list of documents

Each party is obliged to prepare a List of Documents, serving one copy on the other party and lodging a copy with the court. The list should disclose the existence of all documents relevant to the case of both parties, not simply those which support the Plaintiff's case. A typical list in a straightforward debt action will include contract documents, orders, delivery notes, invoices, statements, correspondence and contemporaneous diary notes. These examples are not meant to be exclusive, there will be different relevant documents in each action. The list can either be in a letter or in Form N265, obtainable from the court.

8.3.2   Inspection of documents

When Britannia ruled the waves and a supermarket was where farmers swapped gossip, to produce inspection of documents meant just that, solicitors' clerks poring over yellowing parchment and recording relevant information in laborious copperplate. Today, the photocopier is available. The Plaintiff should check what documents are included in the Defendant's list that he has not seen, or believes may have been doctored, and request copies. The Defendant will do likewise. The party requesting the documents can be charged for reasonable copying expenses. The Plaintiff should not provide copy documents until the Defendant has disclosed his list in case the Defendant endeavours to derive unfair advantage from prior knowledge of the Plaintiff's case.

8.3.3   Witness statements

As any lawyer will confirm, witness statements are complicated. For a litigant in person they are a potential minefield. Statements should be exchanged simultaneously so that one party does not gain any advantage by prior sight of its opponent's evidence. The full name, address and occupation of the person making the statement should be shown and there should follow in full the evidence he will give at trial. The person making the statement should sign and date the statement. All relevant matters should be included. Attempts to call additional undisclosed evidence at trial are liable to be rejected. It is strongly recommended that a litigant in person who finds himself having to prepare anything but the simplest of witness statements should be placing the action in the hands of solicitors.

8.3.4   Request hearing

The automatic directions provide that the trial date be requested no later than six months from the start of the timetable. If the matter is not ready for trial after six months, the Plaintiff should make application to the court for an extension of time before the trial date is fixed. An application with the consent of the Defendant is likely to receive a more sympathetic response from the court.

One major aim of the automatic directions is to prevent parties from dragging their heels in proceeding an action to trial. Any Defendant seeking to delay an action without good reason is likely to receive short shrift from the court.

8.3.5   Striking out action

The danger time is 15 months from the start of the timetable. If by then a trial date has not been requested the case will be automatically struck out. Once this happens the court will not reinstate the case. It is essential therefore to make a diary note to make application for a trial date within the 15-month period. If, approaching 15 months, the action is still not ready for trial, application for extension of the timetable must be made to the court, but further time will only be allowed if good reason can be shown. Arguably, the application should be heard within the 15-month period. Occasions when an extension is necessary will be the exception rather than the rule. One example would be if the Defendant made a late amendment to his defence, raising new issues which obliged the Plaintiff to make amendments to his own pleadings and obtain further information from witnesses on new allegations.

8.3.6 Trial bundle

No later than 14 days before the date fixed for trial, the Defendant advises the Plaintiff what documents it requires to be included in the trial bundle. It is the Plaintiff's responsibility to prepare the bundle. The requirements for the bundle and other documentation to be provided by the Plaintiff are set out on the Notice of Automatic Directions.

Precisely which documents are included in the bundle will depend on the circumstances of any given case. It is sensible in a debt action that the first documents should be the statements of account, followed by invoices and credit notes. The documents usually appear in chronological order but this may be varied to make the bundle easier to follow. For example, a credit note relating to a specific invoice should sensibly follow that invoice even where other documents pre-date it. The bundle should not be padded out with unnecessary documents. Where, for example, the Defendant admits having received the goods, it is unlikely that any useful purpose will be served by including proofs of delivery.

8.3.7 Summary

Of necessity, this is very much an outline survey of the steps required to proceed a matter to trial. Each individual case will throw up its own problems. For a litigant in person not dealing with such matters on a regular basis the process is time-consuming and complex. He may not be acting in his best interests if he attempts to proceed a defended action to trial. Where a defended action is to proceed to trial, the Plaintiff should consider whether to instruct a solicitor.

8.4 Procedure to arbitration

A claim for £3,000 or less will automatically be referred to arbitration once a defence is received. As indicated, a defended claim over £3,000 may be dealt with by way of arbitration on application by either party or of the court's own volition. The final decision is for the court to make. For a litigant in person this more informal procedure is far preferable.

A district judge of the court will determine on the basis of the claim and defence before him whether it is necessary to hold a preliminary hearing in order to give directions prior to the arbitration. Where the district judge considers the standard directions would be inappropriate either because they would be inadequate or he considers the claim to be ill-founded or that no reasonable defence is disclosed, a preliminary appointment may be ordered or he may order non-standard directions of his own volition. Otherwise, for small claims, a notice of the arbitration hearing will be given in the standard form N18A shown at the end of this chapter. A notice in similar form is employed where claims of over £3,000 are referred to arbitration.

As with the automatic directions for trial, the standard form spells out the steps required to bring a matter to arbitration. The requirements are the same for both parties:

(1)   Not less than 14 days before the hearing send the opposing party copies of all documents relied upon to prove the case.

(2)   Not less than seven days before the hearing send to the court and the opposing party a copy of any expert report to be relied upon and the names and addresses of any witnesses to be called.

(3)   Notification is also given of the time, date and length fixed for the arbitration hearing.

The differences in the simplified procedure may be readily appreciated:

(1)   There is no formal process of discovery and inspection of documents, merely the provision of copies to prove the case.

(2)   Whilst any expert reports must be disclosed, witness statements do not have to be exchanged.

The following additional differences should also be appreciated:

(1)   Costs will not normally be awarded for arbitration proceedings.

(2)   Many standard interlocutory procedures do not apply. The most common of these are requests for Further and Better Particulars of a pleading and payments into court.

(3)   The arbitration hearing itself is less formal and less intimidating for a party acting in person. The strict rules of evidence employed in a trial do not apply.

8.5   Summary judgment

Summary judgment is not available for claims of £3,000 or less (ie cases automatically referred to arbitration). It is a useful weapon for a Plaintiff faced with a sham defence. A successful summary judgment application avoids the cost and delay of proceeding to trial. It is appropriate where there is no bona fide defence. The application may be for all or only part of the claim, where, for instance, the maximum value of the sum in dispute can be identified. Where there is a dishonoured cheque from the Defendant, a legitimate defence cannot be raised and a spurious defence will be defeated by summary judgment application.

Application is made by Summons supported by Affidavit. There is no summons fee payable. On the application, the district judge does not try the case, he merely considers whether there is an arguable defence. Summary judgment is not usually appropriate therefore when the central issue is one individual's word against another. In such cases, the district judge is likely to consider that the matter should be determined at trial where witnesses can be cross-examined. The Summons may typically be worded as follows:

IN THE HALIFAX COUNTY COURT   Case No. 957905

BETWEEN

JOHN SMITH t/a WORK SERVICES   Plaintiff

And

A.N. (YORKSHIRE) LTD   Defendant

I wish to apply for Judgment under Order 9 Rule 14 against the Defendant for £3,760.00 and £35.26 interest on the grounds more particularly set out in my Affidavit accompanying this application.

        J. Smith
Signed ....

Plaintiff   13th November 1995

49 Main Street, Halifax

THIS SECTION TO BE COMPLETED BY THE COURT

TO THE Plaintiff/Defendant

TAKE NOTICE that this application will be heard by the District Judge at Prescott Street, Halifax, West Yorks on 11 January 1996 at 3 o'clock.

IF YOU DO NOT ATTEND THE COURT WILL MAKE SUCH ORDER AS IT SEES FIT.

This is on Form N244 but the Plaintiff may as readily prepare his own application provided that the necessary information is included.

The Plaintiff must also prepare an Affidavit, that is a sworn statement. There is no standard form and the Plaintiff must adapt the wording to the facts of each given case. An Affidavit unlike other documents used in proceedings is drafted in the first person singular. The name, address and position of the person swearing the Affidavit ('The Deponent') should appear. Numbered paragraphs should be used. If the Affidavit contains matters outside his direct knowledge, the Deponent should identify why he believes that information to be true. The Affidavit must always include confirmation that the sum claimed is owing, that the Deponent believes that there is no defence to the action and should include a request for summary judgment. Documents in support of the application appear as marked exhibits attached to the Affidavit. Each Affidavit must be marked in the top right-hand corner with the name of the party on whose behalf it is filed, the Deponent's initials and surname, the number of the Deponent's Affidavit and the date of swearing and filing. A basic Affidavit might read as follows:

S Smith: 1
Plaintiff
Sworn: 29/11/95
Lodged: 95
Case No. 957905

IN THE HALIFAX COUNTY COURT

BETWEEN

JOHN SMITH t/a WORK SERVICES   Plaintiff

And

A.N. (YORKSHIRE) Ltd   Defendant

I, SYLVIA SMITH of 49 Main Street, Halifax, West Yorkshire MAKE OATH and say as follows:

1. I am the Plaintiff's Bookkeeper. I make this Affidavit based on my own knowledge and documents placed before me.

2. The Defendant is and was at the beginning of this action indebted to the Plaintiff in the sum of £3,760 as appears from the statement of account produced to me marked 'SS1'.

3. The Defendant claims in its defence that equipment provided by the Plaintiff did not work and was delivered late to the Defendant's site. There is produced to me marked 'SS2' a copy of a letter dated 3 September 1995 in which Mr. Chuzzlewhit of the Defendant company admits the full sum is owing but asks for more time to pay.

4. I verily believe there is no defence to the action.

5. I respectfully submit it is appropriate that the Plaintiff be granted his application for Summary Judgment for £3,760, interest and the court fee.

SWORN at Halifax in the)
County of West York)   }   *Sylvia Smith*
this 29 day of November 1995)

Before me

H. Hornblower

....

Officer of a Court appointed by a Circuit Judge to administer Oaths.

Where there are exhibits, clear photocopies should be employed, and the originals retained. Exhibits may conveniently be attached to an exhibit sheet. This should contain the full details with a heading including the required information in the top right-hand corner. Below the heading the following wording should be inserted:

This is Exhibit 'SS1' of Sylvia Smith sworn before me this 13 day of November 1995.

H. Hornblower
....

Officer of a Court appointed by the Circuit Judge to administer Oaths.

The Affidavit may be sworn before a Solicitor or qualified legal executive, in which case there is a fee payable. An Affidavit for use in a county court action sworn before an officer of the court does not attract a fee.

The Plaintiff should retain a copy of the Summons and Affidavit for his records. The original Affidavit and a copy together with three copies of the Summons should be lodged with the court. The court will need a time estimate for the hearing (five or ten minutes should suffice for a straightforward application). Service of the Summons and Affidavit will normally be effected by the court on the Defendant. They will notify the Plaintiff if they require it to effect service. The Plaintiff will receive back one copy of the application endorsed with the hearing date.

The application and Affidavit must be served on the Defendant not less than seven days before the date fixed for the hearing of the application, otherwise the Defendant will be entitled to an automatic adjournment. He is entitled to file an Affidavit in reply opposing summary judgment. Whether he does or not, he is entitled to attend on the hearing and make representations opposing the application. The hearing takes place before a district judge. The mode of such hearings is set out below at **9.2** 'Interlocutory Applications'.

In outline, the district judge will grant or reject the summary judgment application depending on whether or not the Defendant can show a bona fide defence. If judgment is granted, the Plaintiff can proceed to enforce. If the application is defeated, the case continues as a defended action. Alternatively, the district judge can make an order that the Defendant have conditional leave to defend the proceedings where he considers the defence to be shadowy or is prepared very nearly to give judgment. In such cases, he may typically order that the Defendant have leave to defend provided within, say, 14 days he file at court a fully pleaded defence and/or pay into court all or a substantial part of the claim pending the trial of the action. If the Defendant complies with these conditions the case continues as a defended action. Otherwise, the Plaintiff will be entitled to judgment in default.

8.6 Striking out defence

Any pleading may be struck out under CCR (Ord 13, r 4). Application can be made on notice to the opposing party for the defence to be struck out on the ground that:

(a)   it discloses no reasonable defence; or
(b)   it is scandalous, frivolous or vexatious; or
(c)   it may prejudice, embarrass or delay a fair trial; or
(d)   it is otherwise an abuse of the court process.

Unlike summary judgment, this procedure is not restricted to claims greater than £3,000. If successful in striking out the defence, the Plaintiff may enter judgment without the need to proceed to trial or arbitration.

8.7 Negotiated settlements

Attempts to reach a negotiated settlement can take place at any stage, from before proceedings are commenced right up to the trial or arbitration hearing. They should be considered when a defence is received as there may be a real risk that the defence will be substantially successful. Alternatively, further information regarding the Defendant's financial position may suggest that it would be uneconomical to proceed the matter to trial.

Negotiations may be by letter, telephone or in a meeting. Keep a contemporaneous note of any discussions which will assist if there is a dispute at a later date regarding who said what. If agreement is reached, confirm it in writing. If negotiations are open, however, they can be referred to in future hearings. For this reason, if the possibility of settlement is being explored it may be preferable to mark correspondence 'without prejudice' or as a preliminary to any discussion indicate that the discussion is taking place on this basis. Provided the negotiations are an attempt to achieve settlement, this will render the correspondence or discussions privileged. The terms of privileged documents and discussions cannot be referred to at the subsequent trial or arbitration.

Settlement terms will vary depending on the circumstances of any given case. The negotiations should take place while the proceedings continue. It is important not to allow the Defendant to use the negotiations to delay the case. He should realise that if satisfactory terms cannot be achieved he will face a trial. The following matters should be considered when negotiating.

- If accepting instalment payments, obtain post-dated cheques to avoid having to chase for future payments.
- If the settlement involves the return of goods, who is to pay for their collection?
- In addition to the principal debt the Plaintiff is entitled to court fees paid and interest. Consider also in a defended action the Plaintiff's entitlement to costs.

- Conversely, the Defendant's entitlement to costs also needs to be considered and taken into account in the settlement terms.
- Where there is a counter-claim, the Plaintiff's claim should only be disposed of if satisfactory terms for dealing with the counter-claim have also been agreed.
- Aspects of a claim may be waived, upheld or reduced. Whatever is decided make sure each aspect is provided for.
- The parties may agree that judgment be entered but not enforced provided that the terms of the agreement are upheld. The Defendant is likely to prefer adjournment of the proceedings until the terms are implemented.
- On no account should the Plaintiff agree to dismiss the proceedings until the agreement has been carried through. Otherwise, if the Defendant defaults, the Plaintiff will be obliged to commence another set of proceedings to effect recovery.
- Once terms are agreed, privileged communications become open and should the Defendant then fail to comply with the agreed terms the Plaintiff may seek judgment based on the agreement.

8.8   Discontinuance of proceedings

The defence may disclose issues which convince the Plaintiff that it is inappropriate to continue with the proceedings, for example that payment was made prior to the issue of proceedings but not properly noted due to an error by the Plaintiff. He can then choose to take no action. Under the automatic directions for trial the claim will subsequently be struck out, provided no action is taken by the Plaintiff. This does not apply to cases listed for arbitration. In either event, it is suggested that for clarity and to ensure that court time is not wasted, notice of discontinuance should be filed. Notice should be sent to the court and the Plaintiff should certify that he has given notice to the Defendant. The practice form after the appropriate heading employs the following wording:

NOTICE OF DISCONTINUANCE

TAKE NOTICE, that the Plaintiff hereby wholly discontinues this action as against the Defendant.

....

Dated   The Plaintiff

If the Plaintiff unilaterally discontinues proceedings, the Defendant may be entitled to an order for costs against him. Therefore, a Plaintiff considering discontinuance of proceedings should, before lodging notice, reach agreement with the Defendant in without prejudice negotiations that each party be responsible for its own costs, otherwise he may face a claim for the Defendant's costs.

8.9 Cost considerations

8.9.1 Plaintiff acting in person

A party acting on his own behalf will not be entitled to solicitor's costs. Therefore, the section for solicitor's costs on the summons is left blank. In undefended proceedings, a party acting in person will not be entitled to recover costs from the Defendant, only court fees paid.

A party acting in person who is in receipt of income support is exempt from payment of standard court fees.

Where he is involved in contested proceedings, however, the litigant in person is entitled to recover costs. It seems that this provision applies only to an individual or a partner who is pursuing a debt and not to a limited company. In principle, the litigant in person can recover for work done and disbursements incurred, including payments reasonably made for legal advice. The level at which such costs can be recovered, however, is low.

A party will only be entitled to costs if it is successful in an action. Costs are not usually awarded for a claim of £3,000 or less in any event. The usual order for costs at the conclusion of disputed proceedings is for 'Plaintiff's costs as litigant in person to be taxed in default of agreement'. Without prejudice attempts should be made to agree a figure with the Defendant. In default of agreement, the court will determine an appropriate figure through a taxation procedure. The Plaintiff can enforce the costs order on the same basis as any judgment.

8.9.2 Defendant's entitlement to costs

For claims over £3,000 which proceed to trial, a Defendant who defeats a claim is normally entitled to look to the Plaintiff for his costs. Costs are not usually awarded on Arbitration claims under £3,000. Equally, a Defendant acting in person is only entitled to costs on the same basis as a Plaintiff litigant in person. Where the successful Defendant has instructed a solicitor, he will be entitled to recover the solicitor's costs from the Plaintiff. These are awarded on a higher basis than costs for a litigant in person. Clearly, this is an important factor for a Plaintiff acting in person to determine how and if he should continue with the proceedings.

8.9.3 Legal aid

Legal aid is not available to limited companies, only to individuals. Restricted legal advice is available on a 'Green Form'. A party with a sufficiently good claim but insufficient financial resources may apply through his solicitor for legal aid. Legal aid certificates are available to issue or defend proceedings. A litigant in person is not entitled to a legal aid certificate. If a Defendant obtains a legal aid certificate the Plaintiff should carefully weigh up what future action is appropriate. Costs will not normally be awarded against a legally aided party. Even more seriously, if a Defendant's financial position is so bad that he qualifies for legal aid, what prospect does he have of meeting a judgment?

Flowchart: Defended actions

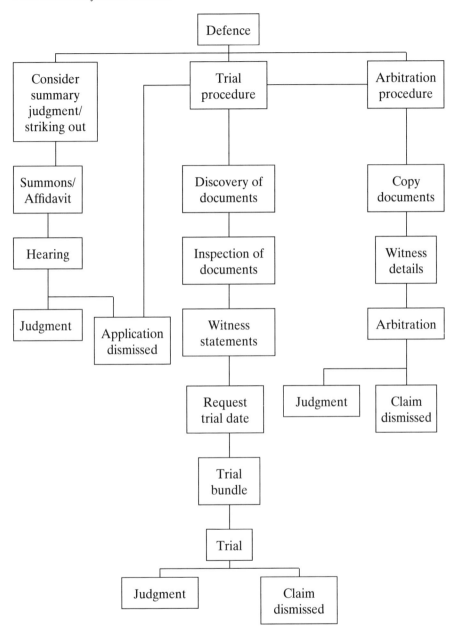

Notice that automatic directions apply (Order 17, rule 11)

	In the
	County Court

Plaintiff

Case No.	

Plaintiff's Ref.	

Defendant

Defendant's Ref.	

Date:	

The court has received a defence in this case which is one to which automatic directions apply.
This means you will not have to come to a court hearing for a District Judge to give directions, that is, to tell you what you have to do to prepare your case for trial. Instead these notes tell you what you must do and the timetable you must follow.
If you want to change any of these directions you must apply to the court.
The timetable begins 14 days after the date given above, or 28 days if a counterclaim was filed with the defence.

Step 1   *(Both parties)*
Not later than **28 days** from start of timetable.

Make a list of all documents you have ever had which contain information about the dispute between you and the other party. You can do this in the form of a letter or use form N265 which you can get from any county court. If the defendant has accepted responsibility for the claim, but is disputing the amount of damages you should receive, only documents relating to the amount of damages need be included in your list. Send your letter (or form N265) to the other party. Tell them where and when they can look at all the documents listed and take copies if they wish. The date(s) you suggest must be within 7 days after the day they get your list. Alternately, the other party can ask you to send them copies of the documents they want. They must ask for these within 7 days of getting your list. You must send the copies within 7 days of receiving their request. The other party must repay you any cost involved e.g. postage, copying charges.

Step 2   *(Both parties)*
Not later than **10 weeks** from start of timetable.

Agree with the other party when you will exchange copies written witness statements (including the written report of any expert witness) you are going to use at the trial. If you don't do this you may not be able to use your witnesses' evidence at the trial. All statements should be signed and dated by the witness. You may not have more than two expert witnesses unless the other party, or the court, agrees.

Step 3   *(Both parties)*
Any time before the start of the trial.

If you are to use photographs or sketch-plans to support your claim, you should, if possible, agree with the other party that they are accurate. The person who took the photographs or made the sketch-plan need not be at the trial.

Step 4   *(Plaintiff only)*
Not later than **6 months** from start of timetable.

Write to the court, asking that a date be fixed for the trial (unless the court has set a date already). Tell the court how long you think the case will last and how many witnesses you and the other party will have at the trial. The court will tell you when the trial will begin, giving you at least 21 days notice.

Step 5   *(Defendant only)*
Not later than **14 days** before the date fixed for trial.

Write to the plaintiff saying what documents you are going to use at the trial.

Step 6   *(Plaintiff only)*
Not later than **7 days** before date fixed for trial

Send the court a bundle of the documents both you and the defendant are going to use at the trial. You should make a numbered list of them, and number each page to correspond with the list. In addition, you should send two copies of the following (if applicable):

- any witness statements (including expert reports) exchanged under Step 2. Say whether or not they were agreed with the other party;
- any legal aid certificate, if not already filed;
- any request for particulars and the particulars given in reply, and the answer to any interrogateries.

Notes

1. **Personal Injury Claims** - In personal injury actions, the Steps are varied as follows:

   Step 1 - Where the injury arises out of a road accident, you need only list documents relating to the amount of damages.
   Step 2 - Each party will be limited to two medical experts and one further expert of any kind unless the parties agree otherwise.
   Step 3 - In an action involving a road accident, you may use any police accident report at the trial without the policeman who made it having to be there. You should agree its contents with the other party if possible.

2. **Changes to the Timetable** - You and the other party may agree a longer period for Steps 1, 2 and 4 but the plaintiff must ask for a date for trial within 15 months from the start of the timetable. If you (the plaintiff) believe you may not be able to request a date within 15 months, you must apply to the court and obtain a new timetable.

3. **Automatic striking out** - if a date for trial has not been requested within 15 months (or within 9 months of the date set for requesting a date for trial given in any new timetable) the case will be automatically struck out and you will not be able to proceed with it.

Notice of Arbitration Hearing

Plaintiff

In the	
	County Court

Case No. *Always quote this*	

Defendant

Plaintiff's Ref.	
Date	

To the plaintiff and defendant

---

1. Details of Hearing

This case is to be dealt with by arbitration under the small claims procedure. The notes overleaf tell you more about the hearing and what you need to do before it takes place.

The arbitration hearing will take place at   County Court

on   , at

The time allowed for the arbitration is   hours,   minutes

If you do not attend, the district judge (the arbitrator) may make decisions in your absence.

If you do not wish your case to be dealt with under the informal small claims procedure, you may apply to the court. You should use form N244 which you can get free from the court office. You must say why you object to your case being dealt with as a small claims case.

The court will give you an appointment at which the district judge will consider your objections. If your case is not dealt with under the small claims procedure, costs may be allowed. That means, if you lose the case you may have to pay the other party's costs which may include the costs of help from a legal representative.

---

2. District Judge's Directions (What you should do)

(i) **Not less than 14 days before the hearing,** you must send the other party a copy of all the documents you have which you are going to use to prove your case.

(ii) **Not less than 7 days before the hearing,** you must send the court and the other party:
(a) a copy of any expert report you are going to use to prove your case and
(b) the name(s) and address(es) of any witness(es) you intend to use.

Notice of arbitration hearing (small claims procedure) (Order 19, Rule 3)   N18A

3. Help and Advice

- You may find it helpful to get advice about your claim and the evidence you should produce at the hearing. Many solicitors will give up to half an hour's advice for a fixed fee of £5, or you may be entitled to advice under the Legal Advice and Assistance Scheme. If expert evidence would help to prove your claim, your local Citizens Advice Bureau may be able to suggest the name of a suitable person to provide a report. They may also offer more general advice and assistance.

- You may take someone with you to the hearing to speak for you. They cannot come to the hearing alone. This person is called a 'lay representative' and can be anyone you choose, for example, your husband or wife, a relative, friend, or advice worker.

- Some lay representatives may want to be paid for helping you. You should make sure you know exactly how much this will be. Consider carefully whether your claim is worth paying that amount. Remember, you will have to pay this yourself.

- You should also remember that some lay representatives who charge for their services may not belong to any professional body. This means that if you are dissatisfied with the way they handle your case, there may be no one to whom you can complain.

- **Small claims leaflet number 6 ('A defence to my claim - what happens now?') and leaflet number 7 (An arbitration hearing - how do I prepare?) will give you more information about the hearing and what you have to do.**

4. Notes on the arbitration hearing

- Arbitration is an informal way of dealing with a claim. The hearing is normally held in private.

- At the hearing the district judge (the arbitrator) will decide on the best way to:
  - identify the facts and matters in dispute, and
  - make sure you have a fair and equal opportunity to present your case.

- The strict rules of evidence will not apply. The arbitrator may take into account any evidence as long as it is fair to both parties to do so.

- If you do not attend the hearing, the arbitrator will normally deal with the case in your absence. But any documents you have sent to the court will be taken into account.

- If you have a lay representative, remember to give the arbitrator form Ex83 at the beginning of the hearing. (The arbitrator can tell your lay representative to leave if he thinks he or she is behaving badly).

- If you do not have anyone to speak on your behalf, you can ask the arbitrator to help by putting questions for you.

- At the end of the hearing, the arbitrator will tell you the decision and the reason for it.

- The decision ('award') made at the hearing is normally final. You can apply to have it set aside, but the grounds (reasons) for doing so are **very limited.**

Chapter 9

HEARINGS

9.1 Types of hearings

In this chapter, we consider some of the hearings that a party acting in person may commonly encounter, how to prepare for the hearing, the format of the hearing and specific considerations to bear in mind when dealing with different hearings.

9.1.1 Procedure

Preparation is vital for all hearings. The importance of keeping a well-organised file has been stressed earlier. Before the hearing, the individual attending should refamiliarise himself with the issues. It pays dividends to make a note of the major points which the party wants to get across at the hearing. If you need to refer to documents, have these readily to hand or suitably marked. It is advisable to be smartly dressed at the hearing because this demonstrates respect for the court. Leave plenty of time for the journey to court. Crimson cheeks and cold sweat are not the best aids to advancing a case.

If you are not familiar with the layout of the court where the hearing is to take place, allow enough time for parking or the journey on public transport. Remember, it may take time to establish just where the hearing is, especially in larger court complexes.

Any party attending at court is recommended to bring with them a supply of change to cover parking fees, drinks from vending machines and any unexpected urgent telephone call. Plaintiffs in person should be prepared to encounter that bugbear for all lawyers, delay. Just because an appointment is listed for 11.00 am does not necessarily mean it will start as advertised. An earlier delay in the list may result in matters running late. Some courts operate a block booking for arbitrations meaning that whilst some will begin at the advertised time, others will be delayed.

The majority of courts operate a system where the parties notify the usher of their arrival as, invariably, he will advise if matters are running late.

What should a Plaintiff in person do if faced with a lengthy delay? The short answer is wait; previous matters may settle and the delay may be shorter than anticipated. Some people suggest reading a book, but it is unlikely that many litigants geared up to the prospect of the hearing will be inclined to curl up with the latest best-selling novel.

Perhaps the only positive way in which this time can be utilised is either through further consideration of the papers or, if the opposing party is present, useful discussions can take place. Ensure that a note of these discussions is taken and if there are possible settlement negotiations that these are conducted on a without prejudice basis.

Apart from trials, the vast majority of applications will be dealt with by a district judge sitting in chambers. The district judge is referred to as 'Sir' or 'Ma'am'. The district judge will not be robed or wear a wig. Hearings in chambers are restricted to the parties and their witnesses; members of the public are not allowed to attend. Hearings take place in the district judge's own rooms. When the usher calls the parties, they will typically find the district judge sitting at his desk with a table extending down at right angles to it. The parties sit on opposite sides of the table.

The district judge will invite the parties to speak. Usually, it is the person making the application who will speak first. It may be that the application is unopposed but, if not, the opposing party will have the opportunity to make his own representations regarding the application. The applicant will be allowed a further opportunity to respond to these points. The district judge may at different times put specific questions to clarify the issue in dispute. Having heard both sides of the case, the district judge will then briefly summarise his findings, give his order and explain the order. A printed copy of the order is then prepared and served by the court.

Anyone attending at a hearing is recommended to bring with them, as well as a calculator, a pen and paper to note important points made by the other side and the district judge. Bear in mind that while the parties may have been living with the case for months, possibly years, the district judge will know nothing of the dispute beyond what appears in the papers before him. Therefore, ensure that he understands the important issues. Explain these in a concise and straight-forward manner and stick to the issues. Be correct and courteous throughout, even if the application is unsuccessful. Interrupting the opponent and hurling unsubstantiated allegations against him are likely to antagonise the district judge. Threatening behaviour and abusive language will not be tolerated. At best, these may result in the application being decided against the offending party; at worst, contempt of court can lead to a fine or short spell in prison.

The issue of costs needs to be dealt with at every hearing. Otherwise, there will be no entitlement at the conclusion of the action to seek costs relating to that particular hearing. In a contested action on a successful interlocutory appli-cation, the Plaintiff should seek an order for 'the Plaintiff's costs of the application as a litigant in person'. If it is unclear at that stage who should have the costs of the day, the district judge may order 'costs in the cause', i.e. to the ultimately successful party, or 'costs reserved'. If the application does not warrant provision for costs, he will either state 'no order as to costs' or be silent as to costs.

9.2 Interlocutory applications

Bear in mind the following points when dealing with interlocutory applications.

9.2.1 Disposal hearings

A disposal hearing occurs when the Defendant offers repayment of the debt by instalments or by lump sum in the future and the offer is unacceptable to the Plaintiff. The Plaintiff makes application by letter or formal application indicating that the Plaintiff does not accept the order made and requesting that the court reviews the position. The hearing will be conducted by a district judge in chambers.

Normally, such applications should only be made where the Plaintiff is able to show that the Defendant has failed to make a full and frank disclosure of its financial position. The Plaintiff may be able to show that income has been omitted or understated or that expenditure has been overstated or includes luxury items. The Defendant should be required to attend on the hearing with documentary evidence to substantiate questionable figures.

The Defendant may be in a position to increase repayments at a later date when, for example, other commitments, such as instalments under an HP agreement cease. Alternatively, the Plaintiff may argue that repayments should be made to it at a higher rate if there are listed court orders against the Defendant under which other creditors are receiving disproportionately high payments.

Disposal hearings are also appropriate where the Plaintiff does not want to be tied to instalment or delayed payments. Therefore, if the Plaintiff can show that other creditors are taking enforcement action and the Plaintiff is therefore being prejudiced, the Plaintiff can seek to have the court order dismissed leaving the Plaintiff free to pursue alternative enforcement action of its own.

Both prior to and at the hearing the Plaintiff should calculate from its own analysis of the Defendant's figures for income and expenditure how much the Defendant can afford to pay. If successful in the application, the Plaintiff is also entitled to ask for the cost of the application. Since, if granted, these amounts are likely to be relatively modest, they should be assessed by the district judge.

9.2.2 Striking out the defence

An application to strike out the defence will usually follow immediately on the service of the defence but there is no reason why it should not be made later if, for instance, the Defendant fails to disclose any documents to substantiate its defence on discovery.

The Plaintiff makes the application to strike out. This should include a request that the Plaintiff be at liberty to enter judgment. The Plaintiff must specify on which ground or grounds it seeks to have the defence struck out. The Plaintiff must satisfy the district judge that such an order is appropriate. The burden is on the Plaintiff to prove that the application should succeed and the court will only order a defence to be struck out in very clear cases. For instance, a Defendant may not deny that the money is owing to the Plaintiff but claim that it is unwilling to pay because its own customer still owes the money. That is no reason for non-payment unless the Plaintiff agreed, unwisely, that its contract with the Defendent would be paid only when settlement was made by the Defendant's customer. If successful, the Plaintiff should ask for costs to be assessed. Prior to the hearing, he should have made a calculation of interest to the hearing date. He should seek judgment for the debt, interest and, if available, costs.

9.2.3   Summary judgment applications

Remember, such applications are only appropriate where automatic reference to arbitration does not apply (see **8.2**). Application is by Summons supported by Affidavit which must be served by the court or Plaintiff no later than seven days before the hearing. If the period of service is less, the hearing will be adjourned until a later date. The Defendant may serve an Affidavit in reply. If the Defendant's Affidavit is received at or immediately before the hearing, it may be appropriate for the Plaintiff to request an adjournment to allow time to investigate the claims made in the Affidavit.

The Plaintiff, as the applicant, first presents his case. He should confirm initially that the district judge has had the opportunity to read all the Affidavits. If the application is unopposed, the district judge may grant summary judgment without going into the matter further. However, even if unopposed, the district judge may still want to be satisfied that the Plaintiff's application has substance. The Plaintiff should first satisfy the district judge that the money is owing. Often this will be by a simple reference to a statement of account.

The Plaintiff will then need to show that there is no valid defence. This may be straightforward where, for example, the defence is no more than a one-line denial. On other occasions, the weakness of the defence will need to be built up, through a series of points, identifying either that the defence is not genuine or restricted at best to part only of the sum claimed. The Defendant may claim that goods supplied were unsatisfactory. Such an argument looks increasingly tenuous the longer the period between delivery of the goods and the complaint. It will assist the Plaintiff attending at the hearing if he prepares beforehand a list of the points to raise. It is all too easy in the heat of the hearing to overlook important points.

If the application is opposed, the Defendant will then have his opportunity to advance his arguments against the application. The Plaintiff's representative should not interrupt the Defendant but note any points made which require expansion or explanation and put these to the district judge once the Defendant has finished his representations.

The district judge will then make his order. If judgment has been granted in whole or in part, interest will be allowed on that sum. The Plaintiff should, therefore, prepare an interest calculation up to the date of the hearing. A prudent Plaintiff will bring a calculator with him. The sum for which judgment is ordered may be less than is hoped. Normally, costs follow the event so that on a successful application the Plaintiff should ask for costs. Costs are always at the court's discretion. A successful Defendant will look to the Plaintiff for costs. The Plaintiff should argue against this if the reason the application failed is that new evidence was advanced by the Defendant at the hearing which was not contained in the original defence. In those circumstances, the appropriate order is 'costs in the cause'. There is also scope for the court to order conditional leave to defend, typically provided that the Defendant makes payment into court to abide the event, that is, pending the outcome of the proceedings.

9.2.4 Application to set aside judgment

It is open for the Defendant to make an application to set aside a default judgment (see Chapter 7) on any date from the date on which judgment was entered. The longer the Defendant delays its application the less sympathetic the court's response is likely to be. Application is made by Summons served by the court on the Plaintiff. The Summons will be endorsed with the hearing date for the application and state that the Defendant applies to set aside all or part of the judgment and set out the grounds relied on. These may be set out in a supporting Affidavit. Applications are normally heard by a district judge in chambers, check the form of notice. However, some courts may list these matters in open court.

A distinction must be drawn between a regular and an irregular judgment. An irregular judgment is defective because it fails to comply with the court rules. If, for example, a Default Summons issued against a Defendant company is served at an address which is not its registered office and does not come to the Defendant's attention, the judgment is irregular and the court will set it aside. Where, however, the Defendant changed its registered office but failed to notify Companies House or the Plaintiff and it does not then receive the Default Summons, the fault is with the Defendant and judgment is regular.

Where judgment is irregular the Defendant will be entitled to have judgment set aside. The district judge will do so without looking into the merits of the defence and the Defendant will be entitled to costs of the application. In such circumstances, it may make sense for the Plaintiff to consent to the order to avoid being further penalised as to costs. The Plaintiff will normally be obliged to further serve the Default Summons in compliance with the court rules before the matter advances. This does not preclude the Plaintiff from making a subsequent application for summary judgment or to strike out the defence where appropriate.

The position is more complicated where judgment is regular. In these cases, the Defendant must satisfy the district judge that it has a defence on the merits with a realistic prospect of success, otherwise the judgment will stand. The Plaintiff must then assess and counter the various arguments put forward by the Defendant.

- 'Judgment is irregular'. The Defendant will often claim this is so when it is not in fact the case. This question needs to be determined before considering the merit of any purported defence.
- 'I don't owe them money'. A mere bald statement will not satisfy the court. The Defendant must give details of its defence. Write to the Defendant

requiring details before the hearing, the Plaintiff is entitled to know what grounds the Defendant relies upon and have time to investigate these. If the Defendant fails to provide requested information, that fact should be drawn to the attention of the district judge. So too should any attempt to spring further details on the Plaintiff at the hearing.

* Nature of the defence. Consider the various standard defences set out at **8.1** and how these may be countered. In particular, the defence may be as to part only, in which case judgment should stand for the undisputed element whilst the disputed balance becomes the subject of contested proceedings.
* Borderline defences. Bear in mind that the district judge can grant leave to defend conditionally where only just satisfied this is appropriate. Typically, this would be conditional on the Defendant making a payment into court to abide the event, pending trial or further determination of the proceedings.

Whilst the Plaintiff will also argue its case before the district judge, it is generally preferable to file and serve an Affidavit in opposition prior to the hearing. Since this is the Defendant's application, he will usually address the district judge first. At the hearing the Plaintiff should list why each of the grounds on which the Defendant relies is inappropriate. Should the Defendant try to introduce new material, the Plaintiff should object to its introduction and, if necessary, seek adjournment to allow time to produce evidence to counter it.

If the district judge determines that judgment should stand, ask for the Plaintiff's costs in person to be assessed and added to the judgment debt. Where the court determines judgment should be set aside, there will need to be provision for a defence to be filed and served, usually within 14 days. This may further be conditional on a payment into court of a specified sum. The Plaintiff will still be entitled to costs of the application in person. If the judgment was regular, fault lay with the Defendant.

9.2.5   Application to stay execution

Check the form of notice, whether the hearing is before a district judge in chambers or in court. Such applications may be made by the Defendant after judgment is obtained, usually in response to attempts to enforce the judgment or where the Defendant claims to be unable to afford to pay the entire judgment immediately and makes the application to pay by instalments or at a future date. The application should state the proposed terms, the grounds on which the application is made and include a signed statement of the Defendant's means. The financial particulars may be by Affidavit or a signed schedule. If either no or incomplete details are provided, the Plaintiff should request these by writing to the Defendant and make further request at the hearing if they are still not volunteered.

The earlier comments regarding the Defendant's ability to pay (see **9.2.1**) are also relevant here. The court will provide a copy of the Defendant's application and statement of means to the Plaintiff. The Plaintiff then has 14 days to notify the court if he objects to the application, providing reasons. In these circumstances the parties will appear before the district judge who will then determine what is the appropriate order to make. The Plaintiff's task will be easier if before the hearing he prepares a list of his objections, including additional knowledge of the Defendant's finances and where he considers full information is not being disclosed. The Plaintiff is being put to additional expense by the Defendant's application and should therefore seek costs.

9.2.6 Application to enforce

A Plaintiff may need to attend court when enforcing a judgment by way of garnishee charging order and oral examination. These are dealt with in Chapter 10.

9.2.7 Appeals

Decisions may be appealed unless the matter has been automatically referred to arbitration. Appeals are, however, very much the exception to the rule. It is suggested that a party contemplating an appeal should seek legal advice. This should be done immediately as strict time-limits apply. It is not appropriate to consider here the appeals procedure in detail but information regarding this should be available from the county court office.

9.3 Final applications

Only where a claim is contested and no settlement proves possible will a matter proceed to a final hearing. Claims referred to arbitration will usually be heard by a district judge in chambers. Otherwise, the matter will be determined by trial in a courtroom. The hearing will be conducted by a district judge or county court judge depending on the size and complexity of the claim and the policy of any given county court. As with all stages of an action, a key element in maximising the prospects for a successful outcome is in thorough preparation for the hearing. Whilst there are procedural differences dependent upon whether a trial or arbitration is to follow, the questions to be asked are essentially the same in both cases.

9.3.1 Preparation for trial

- Plan for the hearing.
- No later than six months from the start of the automatic directions timetable the Plaintiff should write to the court requesting a trial date be fixed, unless the court have already fixed a date. The court should be advised of the estimated length of hearing and number of witnesses to be called.
- Read the court notices. Have they been complied with?
- Take time to go through the Plaintiff's case and establish how this will be proved.
- Undertake the same exercise with the defence. Where this is disputed, how is it to be disproved?
- Documents will be required to prove the Plaintiff's claim. The originals should be taken to the hearing. No later than seven days before a trial the

Plaintiff should lodge at court a bundle of all the relevant documents agreed between the parties for use at the trial. It is suggested at least three copies should be prepared for use by the court, the Plaintiff and the Defendant. A further copy for use by witnesses is of assistance. For ease of reference the pages should be numbered and an index including the page numbers employed. If the Defendant will not agree the bundle the Plaintiff should prepare his own, making it clear to the court that the bundle has not been agreed between the parties.

- Where plans or photographs are submitted in evidence, ensure these are clear and legible.
- There may be witnesses. They can only give evidence of matters within their knowledge. Where a matter is listed for trial no later than 10 weeks from the start of the automatic directions timetable, the parties should exchange written witness statements. Application can be made for more time but a party failing to exchange witness statements runs a real risk of not being able to call that evidence. The statement should cover everything the witness will give evidence on at the trial. The court is entitled to refuse to admit evidence omitted from the witness statement. Copies of witness statements should be lodged at court no later than seven days before the trial and an indication given whether or not these are agreed.
- At a final hearing a witness must give evidence and be available for cross-examination. Affidavit evidence or sworn statements will not be admissible save in exceptional circumstances where, for example, a witness has died or is incapable of attending on health grounds. In such circumstances, the requirements of the Civil Evidence Act 1972 must be complied with.
- Parties may call expert witnesses. Where, for instance, the Defendant claims goods supplied were defective, it may be appropriate for the court to consider independent expert evidence as to whether this is the case. The timetable for expert witnesses is the same as for witnesses of fact. Unless experts' reports are agreed, the parties will wish to call their expert to give evidence at trial.
- No later than seven days before the trial the Plaintiff should lodge with the court any request for particulars and the particulars given in reply and the answer to any interrogatories if these have been raised in the pleadings between the parties.

9.3.2   Preparation for an arbitration hearing

The general considerations listed above apply. The procedure is, however, less formal and the following variations apply:

- Documents should be lodged with the court and served on the Defendant no later than 14 days before the hearing. Whilst there is no formal requirement to prepare a bundle in arbitration for all but the most straightforward applications, the preparation of an agreed bundle will assist all concerned.
- Witness statements need not be filed and served. The only requirement is that no later than seven days before the hearing each party must send to the court and its opponent the name and address of any witness it intends to call.

It is recommended, however, for the Plaintiff's own assistance that a proof of evidence is taken so that the Plaintiff has a record of what the witness will say. An individual presenting the case for the Plaintiff need not furnish his details to the Defendant unless he is to actually give evidence. It is usual for a witness employed by the Plaintiff to use his business rather than home address.

- Not less than seven days before the hearing each party will file with the court and serve on the opposing party a copy of any expert report to be relied upon.
- The court will usually fix the date and length of the arbitration hearing. If the time allowed is insufficient the court should be advised.

9.3.3 Trial

A trial will be held in a courtroom by a judge. There is no jury. For smaller claims the matter may be well be heard by a district judge who should be addressed as 'Sir' or 'Ma'am'. Otherwise, the matter will be heard by a more senior circuit judge who should be addressed as 'Your Honour'. The parties sit on the front row of the seats in the courtroom. It is usual for witnesses to sit behind the party who is instructing them. One party speaks at a time and the judge may interject if he wishes to clarify any points.

The judge will first invite the Plaintiff to present its case. The Plaintiff should take the court through its claim outlining what the claim is in respect of, its amount and the documents (typically invoices and statements of account) verifying the claim. The Plaintiff should then take the court through the remainder of the documentary evidence, identifying the issues between the parties and everything which is relied upon both to support the claim and to cast doubt on the defence. Once the case has been outlined, witnesses should be called.

Each witness gives evidence on oath from the witness box. The witness is first examined by the party who has called him. The opposing party then has the opportunity to cross-examine the witness. It may be that to clarify the position following that cross-examination the Plaintiff may want to re-examine the witness on certain evidence. The Plaintiff should ensure with each witness that he has made a list of the questions he wishes to ask in order to ensure that all of the relevant evidence is placed before the court. Remember, although a witness can re-read his statement before the trial to familiarise himself with the position, he cannot refer to the witness statement when giving evidence. The witness should, however, refer to relevant documents disclosed in the proceedings. Equally, the Plaintiff may wish to refer the witness to allegations raised in the statement from one of the Defendant's witnesses which requires clarification or contradiction.

When the opposing party cross-examines the witness the Plaintiff should make a note of any answers which require clarification and put these to the witness on re-examination.

The Plaintiff should present evidence, both documentary and by way of witness statements, to satisfy the court that the sum claimed is owing and to demonstrate where any defence put forward is not valid. Once the last of the Plaintiff's witnesses has given evidence it is the turn of the Defendant to present its case, indicating to what extent the Plaintiff's claim is disputed and what constitutes the defence to the claim. The Defendant should then take the judge through the documents in support of the defence and examine-in-chief the defence witnesses.

The Plaintiff will already have had the opportunity to consider the Defendant's witness statements. He should have prepared a list of questions he wishes to put to the witness which will expose weaknesses or contradictions in the defence or the unreliability or uncertainty of the witness himself. There may be other matters arising from the witness's examination to be added to that list. The Plaintiff then has the opportunity to cross-examine the witness. Questions should be put firmly but politely. The judge will not tolerate a party badgering the witness. Parties in person stage-struck by the rhetorical flourishes of film and television courtroom dramas are unlikely to find the judge in a patient mood. Following cross-examination the Defendant will have the opportunity to re-examine its witnesses.

Once the last witness has stood down the parties make their final submissions to the court. This should be a brief summary of the main points in favour of the case, including a request for judgment by the Plaintiff. The art of successful advocacy is to encapsulate concisely all the major arguments, to speak clearly and convey a confident grasp of the facts. Depending on the complexity of the issues or the hour of the day the judge may either give judgment there and then with reasons, retire for a period to consider the position before giving judgment or, conceivably, reserve judgment to a future date.

If the Plaintiff's case is good and well prepared, it should succeed, either in full or in part. If so, the Plaintiff should ask for interest to be added to the judgment debt. The Plaintiff should have earlier calculated what interest would be due. If the Plaintiff is successful, he should also request that the Defendant pay the Plaintiff's cost of the action. The usual order would be that the Defendant pay the Plaintiff's costs of acting in person, such costs to be taxed in default of agreement. The Defendant may ask for more time to pay. It is suggested that anything more than payment in full within 14 days should be dealt with in a separate application with the Defendant providing evidence of its financial means.

However, the decision may go against the Plaintiff, in which case the Defendant will be entitled to an order against the Plaintiff for its costs. There is an element of uncertainty in all litigation. For this reason, compromise settlements should never be rejected out of hand. It is this element of uncertainty, allied to the high costs involved, which results in only a small proportion of claims proceeding to trial. Even then it is instructive how many settle outside the doors of the court.

9.3.4 Arbitration

An arbitration will usually be heard before a district judge in chambers rather than the more intimidating atmosphere of a courtroom. Whilst the procedure is slightly more informal, the basic principles of preparation for the hearing and presentation of the parties' cases is very much as set out for the trial.

One major difference is that there is no provision for the parties to exchange witness statements prior to the arbitration hearing. As such, the Plaintiff has no advance warning of what the opposing party's witnesses will say. This means the Plaintiff has both to listen carefully to and note what the defence witnesses say so that their cross-examination is effective. As discussed earlier, costs will not usually be ordered in a matter referred to arbitration.

9.4 Evidence

One aspect of particular concern to litigants in person is how to present evidence, especially at the final hearing of a matter. It is tempting to provide sample dialogue to illustrate how a standard matter might proceed. Regrettably, this would be both artificial and potentially dangerous as each case is different and throws up different factual or legal issues. However, an outline of how best to present a case may assist.

We will consider here both documentary evidence and witness evidence as well as the general presentation of the case. The key to maximising the prospects for success is planning. A Plaintiff in person has often lived with a case for months, possibly years and there is a danger of assuming that the court will know everything about the matter. The court, however, is aware only of what information is produced before it. The Plaintiff must prove its case, otherwise, whatever the moral rights and wrongs, it will not succeed.

A Plaintiff who arrives at the hearing intending to simply recite his story is unlikely to be acting in his best interests. There is also a danger of concentrating solely on the Plaintiff's case and ignoring the issues raised by the Defence or the procedures set out in the court orders. It is essential therefore not only to prove the Plaintiff's case, but also to defeat or at least cast doubt on the issues raised by the Defendant.

Take, for instance, a straightforward claim for goods sold and delivered. The Defendant may, for example, not admit that it received, the goods. If the Plaintiff cannot prove that these were received, there is a real risk the claim will fail. There may be a written proof of delivery, this should be disclosed in the Plaintiff's List of Documents in a trial action (see **8.3.1**), or a copy provided to the Defendant not less than 14 days before the arbitration (see **8.4**), and the proof of delivery produced at the final hearing. However, if there is no document or the proof of delivery is unsigned, it will be necessary to call witness evidence to prove delivery. This may typically be an employee or carrier who delivered the goods to the Defendant, or an employee from whom the Defendant collected the goods at the Plaintiff's warehouse. In an action bound for trial, a witness statement will be required (see **8.3.3**). Where a case will be settled by arbitration, the name and address of the witness must be disclosed not less than seven days before the hearing (see **8.4**).

If at the hearing the Plaintiff fails to produce documentary or witness evidence to satisfy the court that the goods were delivered, the prospects of obtaining judgment are poor. What happens if a Plaintiff attempts to introduce on the day a document or witness not previously disclosed? The failure to comply with the earlier court order means that the court may refuse to admit such evidence. The court rules tend to be more strictly enforced at trials. In certain courts, on an arbitration hearing the district judge may take a more relaxed view about allowing such evidence. However, do not rely on this; the court rules are there to ensure a just and efficient determination of the hearing and should be complied with.

Prior to the hearing, the Plaintiff needs to consider what documents and what witnesses will be required to prove its claim. The same goes for defeating any disputed arguments in the Defence. The Defendant may claim, for example, that the goods were not of the specification ordered. The Plaintiff's case may be that the specification was agreed in a telephone call between the Defendant and the Plaintiff's production manager. The Plaintiff's production manager needs to be at the hearing to give evidence of what was agreed in the telephone conversation.

Otherwise, if the Defendant gives evidence that there was no such agreement it will inevitably carry great weight with the court. It will not be good enough for the Plaintiff's representative to say that the production manager advised him that the specification was agreed. That is hearsay evidence which will not be admitted at trial and either not be admitted or given less weight at an arbitration hearing.

What then of the form of the hearing? It is suggested that the Plaintiff's representative should firstly advise the judge of his name and position with the Plaintiff before briefly outlining the Plaintiff's claim and referring the court to the documents which support the claim. Next, any witnesses in support of the Plaintiff's case should be called to give evidence. At trial, the witness will be sworn in on oath and give evidence from the witness box. On arbitration, the witness sits at the same table as the Plaintiff's representative and some courts dispense with the requirement that a witness gives evidence on oath.

Whilst the arbitration procedure is more informal, the basic structure of giving evidence is the same as at trial. A witness should firstly be asked to confirm his name, address and position with the Plaintiff if employed by the Plaintiff. The examination of the witness proceeds on a question and answer basis. The questions should not be leading questions. For example, the witness may legitimately be asked 'Did you tell the Defendant when you needed the goods?', but not 'You told the Defendant you needed the goods on 11 March didn't you?'.

The witness's evidence should be kept to the important facts and the issues between the parties. Stick to the important points. A witness should not describe everything in a rush. Witnesses, especially at trial, should limit their evidence to what they know, not their opinions on matters or conversations they had no dealings with.

Where there have been without prejudice negotiations in correspondence or in conversations, the substance of these cannot be referred to in evidence. Remember, that unless the Defendant admits it is correct, a witness will be required to prove a document. For example, the Plaintiff's bookkeeper may be the person to confirm that the invoices and statement of account are correct.

9.5 Checklist

(1) Dress in a tidy and respectable manner.
(2) Ensure that you have:
   - all the relevant documents in good order;
   - an extra copy of any essential document;
   - a pen and notebook;
   - a calculator;
   - some change.
(3) Know the whereabouts of the court.
(4) Allow sufficient time before the hearing.
(5) Ensure all court orders have been complied with.
(6) Ensure all witnesses are available to attend.
(7) During the hearing make a note of any relevant submissions by the opposing party.
(8) At a trial or arbitration make a full note of evidence by witnesses.
(9) Make a verbatim note of any judgment or order and check this with the sealed copy subsequently received from the court.

Chapter 10

ENFORCEMENT

Plaintiffs in person sometimes mistakenly suppose that judgment represents the conclusion of proceedings. Judgment is in fact an order of the court requiring the Defendant to make payment. If the Defendant fails to make payment, the Plaintiff should pursue enforcement action provided it believes that the Defendant has the ability to make payment.

The enforcement options are the same whether judgment was obtained on a default basis, through the defence being struck out, summary judgment application or following a full trial or arbitration. The options available are:

(1) warrant of execution;
(2) oral examination;
(3) attachment of earnings;
(4) charging orders;
(5) garnishee orders;
(6) insolvency proceedings.

10.1 Warrant of execution

10.1.1 Warrant of execution

Since a warrant of execution is by far the most common enforcement remedy, it is considered here in far greater detail than the other enforcement options. To apply for a warrant, there must be an unsatisfied judgment and, either, no order for instalment payments or, if such an order exists, the Defendant must be in default. A warrant is an appropriate enforcement option in virtually all instances. The court bailiff attends at the Defendant's premises and is empowered to seize and sell the Defendant's goods if payment is not made.

Application for a warrant can be made at any time following the entry of judgment and, indeed, is usually made at the same time as the application for judgment. Execution against goods pursuant to an agreement under the Consumer Credit Act 1974 must be by way of warrant of execution, whatever the size of the claim. For all other claims, however, where the value of judgment is below £2,000, execution must be by way of warrant. From £2,000 to £4,999.99, execution may be by way of either warrant or High Court execution. Judgments of £5,000 and more must be enforced in the High Court. High Court enforcement is discussed later.

Whilst it has many advantages for legal practitioners, High Court execution is technically quite complex and for judgments of between £2,000 and £5,000 county court warrants are recommended for Plaintiffs acting in person. The request for warrant of execution is made by a standard form, forwarded to the court with the appropriate fee. An example of the appropriate form is shown at the end of this chapter. The remainder of the information, including the warrant number, will be inserted by the court. The balance on the judgment is inserted allowing credit for any payments made. Interest following judgment is not allowed where judgment is for less than £5,000. The issue fee is currently £20 for judgments not exceeding £125 and £40 for judgments exceeding £125. Where application is made by post a self-addressed reply envelope should also be provided. If the Plaintiff is aware of any specific assets belonging to the Defendant which the court might not otherwise identify it can, at any time, advise the court of these.

Enforcement of the warrant of execution is undertaken by the county court. Where the defendant's address is within the jurisdiction of the county court in which judgment was obtained, that court will effect enforcement. Where the Defendant lives or trades elsewhere, the original county court will forward the warrant to the county court having jurisdiction for that address. This is known as the local county court. The original county court will inform the Plaintiff of the warrant number and whether the warrant has been forwarded to a local county court. If that is the case, the court will advise the local number for the warrant in due course. The Plaintiff should quote the case number, warrant number and, where appropriate, local number to ensure that its correspondence is promptly dealt with. It is a regrettable fact that the courts are under severe pressure of work. It is recommended that, if confirmation of the warrant number, is not received within 14 days, the Plaintiff should chase for this and send regular reminders to the court if not fully updated on the warrant's progress.

The court should keep the Plaintiff advised of the enforcement action being taken. Plaintiffs should note that if a warrant has not been executed within one month the court must then, and every subsequent month while the warrant remains outstanding, send to the Plaintiff notice giving the reason for non-execution. If the Plaintiff seeks clarification of the position and cannot obtain a satisfactory response to correspondence, the Plaintiff can telephone the bailiff section of the relevant county court. Usually, the best time to catch the bailiffs at court is before 10.00 am. Where a local county court is enforcing, writing to them direct will cut down delays.

Warrants are enforced by the county court bailiffs. The court rules provide that the bailiff should, as soon as possible, obtain payment which will be forwarded via the court to the Plaintiff. If payment is not made, the bailiff levies on sufficient of the Defendant's goods to satisfy the warrant, together with the costs of removal and sale. If this is the case, the bailiff either removes the Defendant's goods to a sale room or enters into a walking possession agreement with the Defendant. Under such an agreement, the Defendant, pending satisfaction or withdrawal of the warrant, will not remove or dispose of goods levied upon. If the Defendant subsequently breaches the walking possession agreement he will be in contempt and liable to be penalised by the court.

The timetable envisaged on the reverse of the warrant of execution is rarely followed in practice. This may be because over-worked court bailiffs have not been able to deal with the warrant. Alternatively, they may be denied access by a recalcitrant Defendant. The bailiffs cannot force access at domestic premises. They may do so, however, at a business address. In those cases, they will write first to the Plaintiff for authority to take such action, seeking an indemnity for the additional costs incurred in the event.

Often the bailiff will have prior warrants for the same Defendant. Warrants are enforced in strict chronological order although a distress warrant for unpaid rent or rates may enjoy priority. If there are prior warrants to that of the Plaintiff in the event of a forced sale of the Defendant's goods, the prior execution creditors will take from the net proceeds of the sale. The Plaintiff may, therefore, have to wait in line if the Defendant is making instalment payments to the prior creditors in the hope of an improved realisation at a future date.

As indicated, even if there are no warrants in priority to that of the Plaintiff, the Defendant may not be able to pay the sum claimed and the Defendant's assets may be of insufficient value to justify their removal for sale. In these circumstances, the Plaintiff may consider it expedient to accept an offer of instalment payments from the Defendant. If a subsequent execution creditor forced a sale of the Defendant's goods, the Plaintiff would still benefit to their limited value.

When accepting instalment payments or waiting for prior execution creditors to be paid, the Plaintiff should make a diary note that the warrant is only valid for 12 months from issue. If, before the end of that period, all or part of the judgment debt remains outstanding, the Plaintiff is entitled to make an application to the court to renew the warrant for a period of up to 12 months. The application should be made before the initial 12 months expires. Applications after that date are at the discretion of the court. Renewal of the warrant preserves the Plaintiff's priority against other execution creditors. It is open for the Plaintiff to issue second and subsequent warrants within six years of judgment, or later with the consent of the court. A new warrant would not, however, preserve the Plaintiff's priority against other execution creditors. In default of payment, if he has identified goods of sufficient value belonging to the Defendant, the bailiff will arrange for removal of the Defendant's goods. Items necessary for personal use in business as well as clothing, bedding and furniture and provisions necessary for basic domestic needs are exempt from seizure as well as money and cheques. Whilst the bailiff may arrange for private sale of specialist items, it is more usual for a Defendant's goods to be sold by way of auction sale. Plaintiffs and Defendants alike will appreciate that the full value of goods is rarely realised on forced sale.

Expenses are first deducted from the proceeds of the auction sale. Any surplus will be available to the execution creditors in order of priority. Where a warrant is issued for a judgment exceeding £500, all monies paid, either by the Defendant to avoid a forced sale or as proceeds of sale, are retained by the court for 14 days before being forwarded to the Plaintiff. If during that period, a bankruptcy order or winding-up order (for individuals or companies respectively) is made, the court is obliged to forward payment instead to the Defendant's trustee in bankruptcy or liquidator. The mere fact of being an execution creditor does not entitle the Plaintiff to any more privileged position in the insolvent estate.

It is worth summarising some of the common ways in which a warrant of execution develops.

- The Defendant pays. The matter is at an end.
- The Defendant makes no payments and has no goods of value which the Plaintiff can identify. The options are:
  - Withdraw the warrant. Write off the debt.
  - Direct the bailiff to other known assets.
  - Take alternative enforcement action.
- The Defendant offers instalment payments and has no goods of value which the bailiff can identify. The options are:
  - Accept instalment payments.
  - Attempt to negotiate improved payments.
  - Direct the bailiff to other known assets.
  - Take alternative enforcement action.
- Whether or not the Plaintiff rejects an offer of delayed or instalment payments by the Defendant, it is open for the Defendant to make an application for stay of execution to the court.
- No payment by the Defendant who has goods of value. In such circumstances, the bailiff should be instructed to remove and sell the Defendant's goods.
- The Defendant offers payment by instalments and also has goods of value. In each instance, it must be for the Plaintiff to determine whether the offer is acceptable or to instruct the bailiff to proceed to a forced sale. It is still open for the Defendant to apply for a stay of execution.
- A third party claims the Defendant's goods. The options are:
  - Admit third party claim. The same options are then available as if Defendant has no goods.
  - Dispute third party claim in interpleader proceedings. If successful, the same options are available as if Defendant has goods.
(Third party claims are discussed in greater detail below.)
- Prior execution creditor(s). Defendant has no goods. The options are:
  - Wait in line if Defendant making instalment payments.
  - Withdraw the warrant and write off the debt.
  - Attempt alternative enforcement action.
- Prior execution creditor(s). Defendant has goods. The options are:
  - If goods of insufficient value, options as above.
  - If goods of sufficient value, additional option of instructing bailiff to effect a forced sale.

10.1.2 Third party claims

The bailiff can only seize and sell goods belonging to the Defendant to satisfy the warrant. He may attend at the Defendant's address and a third party may claim that goods seized belong to them, not the Defendant. The Plaintiff should inform the bailiff within four days whether he admits or opposes the third party claim.

If the third party claim is admitted, the bailiff will not be able to look to those goods to satisfy the Plaintiff's warrant. If the third party claim is disputed, a second set of interpleader proceedings are instituted to determine who has title to the goods. If the Plaintiff is successful in those proceedings in satisfying the court that the goods do belong to the Defendant, the bailiff may seize and then sell the goods to satisfy the warrant. Otherwise, the bailiff cannot seize and sell the goods.

Interpleader proceedings pose two main problems for the Plaintiff. The first is evidence. The Plaintiff may suspect, but almost certainly will not know, whether or not the third party claim is bogus. The Defendant is unlikely to volunteer assistance. The Defendant and third party may be conspiring together to prevent the Defendant's assets from being taken and sold. The claimant must produce evidence to support his claim in the proceedings but by this stage the Plaintiff has already incurred a risk as to costs. Costs are the second problem area. They can be high, and an unsuccessful Plaintiff will usually be obliged to pay the costs of the successful third party and the court. Given their uncertainty in costs, practitioners often recommend admitting a third party claim rather that becoming embroiled in interpleader proceedings, and attempting to effect recovery through alternative enforcement action.

What then are likely claims that the Plaintiff may encounter and how are these best addressed?

- Jointly owned goods, eg owned by husband and wife, or Defendant and business partner. The goods may be seized and sold with the proceeds to be divided between the co-owners according to their share.
- Spouse or other family member claims title to the goods. Such claims can be difficult to disprove.
- Third party claims to goods of limited value. These should invariably be admitted on economic grounds.
- Claims by HP or finance leasing companies. If these are over items commonly subject to such agreements, eg office equipment and vehicles etc, it is probable such claims are genuine and can be backed up by documentary evidence.
- Claims by an unpaid supplier relying on retention of title to its goods. Again, such claims are likely to be capable of substantiation.
- Another business claims to have taken over from or to be operating at the same address as the Defendant. Perhaps this is genuine, especially if the Plaintiff's own information is out of date, but it may be a try on. Check the claimant's letterheading. Is this a genuine third party or some creation by the Defendant to throw creditors off the scent?
- Beware of Defendants operating a multitude of trading styles. The Plaintiff may issue against an individual trader or a limited company only to find that goods identified by the bailiff are claimed by a sister company which the Plaintiff knows is controlled by the same people. The bailiff cannot remove

these goods as they are claimed by a separate legal entity. The Plaintiff must determine whether to admit the claim or dispute it and enter into interpleader proceedings.

10.1.3 Execution in the High Court

A county court judgment (not subject to a regulated agreement under the Consumer Credit Act 1974) of £5,000 and over *must* be enforced in the High Court, whereas a county court judgment from £2,000 to £4,999.99 *may* be enforced in the High Court.

The county court provides the sealed and signed Certificate of Judgment to the Plaintiff. The Plaintiff must then either write to or attend at the High Court office. There are District Registries of the High Court throughout England and Wales and, save in London, the High Court is usually under the same roof as the county court.

The High Court registers the judgment and assigns an action number in the High Court. There is no fee payable. The Plaintiff prepares a request for and Writ of Fieri Facias (Fi Fa) for the court to issue and seal. The fee payable is currently £20. The court office then return the Fi Fa to the Plaintiff who forwards it plus a fee of £2 + VAT for execution to the under sheriff of the county in which the Defendant trades or resides. The under sheriff forwards the Fi Fa to the sheriff's officer for a given area. Communication regarding the enforcement is between the Plaintiff and the sheriff's officer.

The principles governing enforcement in the two courts are largely similar. The major perceived differences are in cost and efficiency. The county court bailiffs are civil servants who are employed and paid by the court, and they are frequently overworked. The sheriff's officers are, by contrast, paid by results. It is in their interest, like the Plaintiff, that the enforcement action is successful. Generally, their reporting time is quicker. While they are perceived by legal practitioners to be more efficient they are also, however, more expensive.

Generally, when a warrant of execution is issued the Plaintiff will pay no more than its fee. On the rare occasions when there are additional charges, the court will notify and seek authority from the Plaintiff before that expense is incurred. In High Court executions, the sheriff's officer is entitled to payment on a scale of charges including poundage and an inventory fee. In addition, he may incur expenses, for example removal expenses. If the enforcement action is successful and the sheriff's officer is able to recover his fees from the Defendant, their extent is of no immediate concern to the Plaintiff. Where, however, for whatever reason, the sheriff's officer cannot recover his fees from the Defendant, he is entitled to look to the Plaintiff for payment. Depending on the amount of work done, the fees can range from a nominal amount to hundreds of pounds and, potentially, more.

Whilst enforcement in the High Court may be appropriate for larger debts, further details regarding the procedures are not given here. This book concentrates on recovery action in the county court. For a Plaintiff in person the set fees and pre-printed forms make the county court more readily accessible and understandable. The Plaintiff should, however, be aware of the High Court enforcement option and its perceived greater efficiency. If that is the ultimate aim, it is suggested that it would be better to institute proceedings in the High Court in the first instance and instruct a lawyer for this purpose.

10.2   Oral examination

Oral examination is not strictly a method of enforcement. It is a means of obtaining further information regarding the Defendant's financial position. Application can be made at any time from the entry of judgment, and could be employed immediately or following an unsuccessful warrant of execution.

Where the Plaintiff wishes to apply for oral examination and the debtor's address is within the jurisdiction of the court, the Plaintiff should request in writing to the original court for transfer of the action to the Defendant's home court. The transfer is arranged by the two courts. Similar provisions apply when making application for an attachment of earnings order and a charging order.

The Plaintiff files with the court a request for oral examination and the fee payable, currently £30.

Where application is made by post the Plaintiff should also supply a self-addressed reply envelope. Where judgment is for more than £5,000 and interest is being claimed, two copies of the certificate of judgment giving interest details should be provided. The Plaintiff may request conduct of service of the papers but it is usual for this to be left with the court, at least in the first instance.

A completed copy of the request, Form N316, is shown at the end of this chapter. The Plaintiff must certify the balance now due on the judgment. Any credits to be allowed or interest added should be referred to in the outstanding debt section. The person to be examined will either be an individual Defendant, one of the partners where the Defendant is a firm or, in the case of a limited company, a director. Not only must the individual attend the hearing appointed by the court, he must also produce at the examination any relevant books or documents.

The court will fix the hearing date perhaps six to eight weeks hence, notifying the Plaintiff, and effect postal service on the individual to be examined. Some courts prefer to allow the debtor the chance to complete the questionnaire before making the order for examination. If the Plaintiff is not satisfied by the information provided, the Plaintiff may require the examination to proceed in any event. The examination takes place before an officer of the court, the debtor answering questions is put on oath. The examination takes place in the debtor's local county court. The examining officer records the debtor's evidence and both he and the debtor sign the completed depositions.

Should the Plaintiff attend at the oral examination hearing? The Plaintiff should first discover what is the practice of that particular county court as practice does vary from court to court. Some courts will not proceed unless the

Plaintiff is also represented at the hearing. If the court does not advise the Plaintiff to attend, does he want to? A businessman in Berwick is unlikely to make a trek to, say, Plymouth County Court unless he has to. Quite apart from the inconvenience, there is no guarantee that the debtor will attend.

These provisos apart, where it can readily be done, it is recommended that the Plaintiff attend at the oral examination hearing. The Plaintiff will have the opportunity of putting questions to the debtor. These can cover all aspects of the Defendant's financial position and should include:

• Full name and address;
• Employed/self-employed;
• Details of dependants;
• Rent/mortgage;
• Hire purchase/court orders/essential regular payments;
• Vehicles;
• Items of value;
• Property details;
• Bank/building society account details;
• Furniture;
• Stocks and shares;
• Endowment insurance policies.

In addition, where the Defendant is employed, the following information should be sought:

• Employer's name and address;
• Unemployment details;
• Job;
• Works reference;
• Earnings basic/overtime;
• Other income;
• Spouse's earnings;
• Benefits/pension received;
• Details of existing attachment of earnings orders.

Where a Defendant is self-employed, the following details should be sought:

• Self-employed monthly earnings;
• Business address;
• Details of existing contracts;
• Business assets;
• Business bank account details.

Bear in mind also the requirement that the debtor must attend with any relevant books and documents. These can include, for example, business accounts, bank statements, confirmation of mortgage details and vehicle ownership. Where the Plaintiff is interested in particular documents, he should write to the debtor requiring these to be brought to the hearing. The need to produce documentary evidence can assist in tying down an evasive debtor. There is a discretion whether to allow very limited costs of examining the debtor to a Plaintiff's solicitor but it does not seem that a Plaintiff in person would benefit from this provision. The absence of provision for payment of the Plaintiff's costs is one negative aspect of the oral examination procedure.

As indicated, the debtor may fail to attend at the initial hearing, an adjourned hearing may follow. Some courts require the Plaintiff to request this, then the court will fix a new hearing date. Service must be personal, no later than ten days before the adjourned hearing, and will be by the court bailiff or, if so requested, by the Plaintiff himself. It is recommended that the Plaintiff arrange for service only if the bailiff is experiencing difficulties and the Plaintiff is satisfied that the debtor is taking steps to evade service. If requested by the debtor, the Plaintiff's representative must pay conduct money that is sufficient for travelling expenses to the court.

What happens if the debtor fails to attend at the adjourned hearing? There is provision for a further hearing before the judge and, in extreme cases, where the debtor again fails to attend, there is provision for the debtor's committal to prison for a short period for contempt of court.

From the Plaintiff's point of view, oral examination can prove more useful in theory than it does in practice. In successful cases, it may result in identification of information to enable alternative enforcement action. However, against a 'professional' Defendant, it can prove a blunt instrument and a time-consuming one at that. The debtor may not attend or only pay lip service to the procedure by furnishing information which the Plaintiff knows but cannot prove to be either false or incomplete. Rather than following the oral examination procedure to the bitter end, the Plaintiff may be better advised to consider another of the enforcement options. Plaintiffs, and indeed Defendants, should bear in mind that giving of false information on oath is perjury which may render the debtor liable to a fine or imprisonment by the court. Be aware both of oral examination's uses and its limitations.

10.3   Attachment of earnings

Application for an attachment of earnings order can be made at any time after judgment has been obtained. As the description implies, it cannot be enforced against a self-employed Defendant and its application is limited to a Defendant in paid employment. In addition, certain pensions can be attached but not the guaranteed minimum pension or pension payable in respect of disability or any enactment relating to social security.

The Plaintiff files at court a request for an attachment of earnings order together with the fee payable, currently £50. A self-addressed reply envelope should be provided where the application is by post. Where appropriate, two copies of a certificate giving details of interest on judgments over £5,000 should be provided.

The request is made on Form N337, a completed example of which is shown at the end of this chapter. As with a request for oral examination, the Plaintiff must certify the amount outstanding on the judgment. The Plaintiff may not have full information at section 6 regarding the Defendant's employment. Obviously, whatever information can be provided will assist the Plaintiff's case.

How does the Plaintiff establish details of the Defendant's employment? This may be as a result of long-standing knowledge of the Plaintiff, enquiries more recently made or following from oral examination. Another possibility is for the Plaintiff to lodge a request for a search of the court's attachment of earnings index (Form N336) which will reveal whether any existing attachment of earnings orders are in place. There is no fee payable.

The court will issue a notice of application for an attachment of earnings order, serve the Defendant and advise the Plaintiff the application has been issued and the attachment of earnings number which should be quoted in all future correspondence. Form N56 is reproduced at the end of this chapter. This statement of means should be completed by the Defendant and returned to the court. The court should provide a copy of the completed statement of means to the Plaintiff. The Defendant has eight days from service in which to reply.

On return of the statement of means, it is usual for an officer of the court to make an order fixing the Defendant's protected earnings rate and normal deduction rate without attendance by the parties. The protected earnings rate is that below which the Defendant's earnings should not fall. It takes into account the Defendant's commitments as set out in his statement of means. If the Defendant's actual earnings subsequently reduce, this can result in a reduction in the normal deduction rate, that is the monthly sum payable to the Plaintiff. Alternatively, the order may be made by a district judge without attendance by the parties, or at a hearing where the parties may attend. An example of an attachment of earnings order Form N60, is reproduced at the end of this chapter, although not the reverse sheet, which is a record of payments. In fact, it is common for payment to be made by the Defendant direct to the Plaintiff under a suspended attachment of earnings order. Only if payments fail under the suspended order is a fully fledged attachment then made with payments from the employer to the court and thence to the Plaintiff. The suspended order has the advantage of the Defendant's position not being disclosed to his employer and, presumably, jeopardising that job. Where more than one creditor applies, the court will make a consolidated attachment of earnings order, splitting payments on a pro rata basis.

Either party may object to the attachment of earnings order, notifying the court and the other side. Objections should be lodged within 14 days. The court will then fix an appointment where both parties will make representations to the district judge in chambers, who will either endorse the original order made or amend it. Inevitably, Defendants' applications tend to seek a reduction in the normal deduction rate whilst those by Plaintiffs attempt to increase that figure. To do so successfully the Plaintiff must show either that on the figures the Defendant can afford to make repayments at a higher level or persuade the court that certain of the expenses should either not be allowed or are artificially high.

A problem frequently encountered in applications for an attachment of earnings order is that the Defendant fails to return the statement of means form. The court issues a new order for production of statement of means. This is personally served by the bailiff. The Defendant has eight days from service to return the completed statement of means. In default the Defendant may be ordered to attend before the court and committed to prison for up to 14 days or fined up to £250. The bailiff may experience difficulties in effecting service on the Defendant. The Plaintiff should advise the court to serve the Defendant at the place of his employment. There is provision for the Plaintiff to attempt to affect service if the bailiff continues to experience difficulties.

Attachment of earnings can prove a useful remedy, especially when the sum owing is relatively low and the Defendant's earnings are high. For larger debts, however, it only provides a relatively long-term solution and, as such, is unlikely to be attractive. Consider also the problems which will arise if the Defendant loses or changes employment. Whilst legislation provides that the Defendant should notify new employment details, in practice he may not do so. Where the application is successful, the fee paid should be added to the judgment debt. Whilst experience varies from court to court, there are certainly instances of long delays in the administration of applications for an attachment of earnings order. Plaintiffs should make regular diary notes to obtain updates from the court.

10.4 Charging orders

A charging order will not itself result in early payment of a judgment debt. It is a charge over securities, for example stocks and shares or, most usually, a Defendant's interest in land. The charging order provides a measure of security, although not as watertight as a mortgage. The charging order may result in payment of the judgment on the Defendant's death or when he sells his interest in the property. A charging order does not result in a forced sale of the property, a further set of proceedings are required for this.

The long-term nature of the charging order makes it more attractive to financial institutions. By and large, trade creditors cannot afford to take such a long view. For this reason charging orders are not considered here in such detail as other more immediate enforcement remedies. That does not mean, however, they should be ignored, charging orders form a valuable weapon in the legal armoury. They can be pursued for their own sake, either as a first option or when other possibilities have been exhausted. Alternatively, they can be used, say, in conjunction with an attachment of earnings order. If the Defendant is unlikely to afford more than relatively nominal payments, a charging order will provide a measure of longer-term security. Remember, though, that a charging order is not available if the Defendant is complying with an order for instalment payments, including by way of attachment. If, therefore, such a dual course is to be followed the charging order should be obtained before beginning the attachment application.

In outline, how does a Plaintiff advance a charging order application? Again, it is a remedy only available from judgment onwards. The first problem is to establish whether the Defendant has an interest in the property. Such information may be revealed on an oral examination. A quicker and surer method is to search for the information. The vast majority of property in England and Wales is now registered land, the title details are administered by regional offices of HM Land Registry. Anyone can search on standard forms, on payment of a current fee of £10, to establish whether a Defendant is joint or sole owner of a given property. The office copies returned will reveal who owns property and when they bought it, as well as particulars of mortgages affecting the property. There is no information regarding what the property is worth or the amount outstanding on mortgages. The Plaintiff must judge if he believes the Defendant has any financial interest in the property once those mortgages are discharged. There is a risk that property is charged to the hilt or that there is negative equity.

Having established the Defendant's interest in the property the Plaintiff makes application to the court by way of Affidavit, with a self-addressed reply envelope and a cheque for the fee, currently £25. The Affidavit should include details of the judgment, the balance outstanding, and confirm the Defendant's interest in the property, usually exhibiting the office copy entry. The application is lodged with the court office who will refer it to a district judge. Provided he is satisfied the application is in order he will make a charging order nisi. A sealed order will be provided by the court to the Plaintiff.

One advantage of this procedure is that it operates ex parte, ie without notice to the Defendant. It is for the Plaintiff to serve a sealed copy of the charging order nisi and supporting Affidavit on the Defendant and any other party required by the court. Unless service is acknowledged, the court are likely to require a further Affidavit as proof of service. The Plaintiff should take immediate steps to register an appropriate entry at the Land Registry, or Land Charges Department for unregistered land, to protect its position. Otherwise, the charging order will not be effective against third parties seeking to buy or create charges over the property.

Charging orders, like divorce, come in two stages. The order nisi will be endorsed with a hearing date where the charging order may be made absolute. The hearing takes place before a district judge in chambers. The Defendant or any other party interested in the land may attend and oppose. The Plaintiff should attend to obtain the charging order absolute. The Plaintiff should also ask for fixed costs and disbursements of the application. If the district judge is satisfied, the order absolute will be made and the court will provide a sealed order to the Plaintiff who should arrange for service on any interested party not already served by the court. Practice varies, but many practitioners also register the order absolute. Once a charging order absolute is obtained most mortgage holders will disclose the amount owing to them.

Any Plaintiff contemplating a charging order as a means of enforcing a judgment but not confident regarding the procedure, might consider referring the action to a solicitor.

10.5 Garnishee orders

Garnishee orders cover situations where a third party, known as the garnishee, owes money to the Defendant. For example, the Plaintiff may be aware that the Defendant holds money in a bank account, or discover that a customer of the Defendant owes money to it on either a regular contract or for goods supplied. The purpose of the order is to require the garnishee to pay the money to the Plaintiff. Application can be made at any time following entry of judgment with the usual proviso that if any order for instalment payments was made, the Defendant must be in default under this before enforcement action is available.

The Plaintiff is most likely to discover information regarding the garnishee either as a result of an oral examination or through the Plaintiff's own dealings with the Defendant. The garnishee is typically either a customer of the Defendant or a bank or building society where the Defendant holds an account.

Application is made after obtaining judgment. The procedure followed is similar to that for a charging order. The Plaintiff forwards to the court an Affidavit, together with a self-addressed reply envelope and a cheque for the fee, currently £30. A sample Affidavit is shown below. It must include judgment details and certify the balance owing giving details of the proposed garnishee who must live or trade within England or Wales. The grounds for believing the sum of money is owing must be stated. Relevant branch and account number details should be inserted if known.

R Hood No 1
Plaintiff
Sworn 5th May 1995
Lodged 5 May 1995

IN THE NOTTINGHAM COUNTY COURT   Case No NG111111

BETWEEN

RICHARD PLANTAGENET LTD   Plaintiff

and

JOHN PLANTAGENET   Defendant

I, ROBIN HOOD of Sherwood Forest Road, Nottingham, Managing Director of the Plaintiff Company MAKE OATH and say as follows:

1. That on the 13th day of February 1995 the Plaintiff obtained judgment in this court against the above-named Defendant for the sum of £1,750 for debt and costs.

2. That the said sum of £1,750 is still due and unpaid under the judgment.

3. That to the best of my information and belief the Garnishee, Sheriff Knot Bank Limited of Castle Buildings, Nottingham is indebted to the Defendant in the sum of £2,000. The reasons of my information and belief are that the Defendant so advised when orally examined before this court on the 20th day of April 1995.

4. That the Garnishee is a deposit-taking institution having more than one place of business and the name and address of the branch at which the Defendant's account is believed to be held is 5 Maid Marian Crescent, Nottingham. The number of the account is believed to be 54321.

5. The last known address of the Defendant is 18 The Tower, London EC2.

SWORN at Nottingham in the ⎫
County of Nottinghamshire   ⎬   R. Hood
This 5 day of May 1995   ⎭

Before me, G Gisbourne
Officer of the Court, Appointed by
The Judge to take Affidavits.

The garnishee application is referred to the district judge who will make a garnishee order to show cause within, say, five days provided everything is in order. The order to show cause is prepared by the court. It recites the debt owing and orders the garnishee to attach so much of the money as is owing by it to the Defendant to satisfy the debt. The hearing date is endorsed, typically six to eight weeks hence, when the order will be made absolute unless a party can show good reason why this should not be the case.

The beauty of the procedure is that neither the Defendant nor the garnishee is aware of what is going on. This element of surprise will hopefully prevent monies from being transferred to defeat the application. A sealed copy of the order is served on the Plaintiff. The court will serve the garnishee by post, serving a copy at least seven days later on the Defendant so that the Defendant does not have prior knowledge. If the Plaintiff has doubts over service on the garnishee, the Plaintiff may request that it effects service.

10.6 Insolvency proceedings

Insolvency proceedings remain the ultimate sanction available to creditors. They are both expensive and technically complex. As such they are not dealt with here in detail but some outline consideration of the principles and procedures involved will assist in providing a full picture.

Winding-up petitions are issued against limited companies, bankruptcy petitions are issued against individuals. A winding-up petition may be issued against a partnership and bankruptcy petitions against the partners. Insolvency proceedings are only appropriate for undisputed debts of £750 or more. They may be issued either following judgment or as a separate set of proceedings in their own right. One element in the high cost stems from the Official Receiver's deposit payable on presentation of the petition, currently £300 on the bankruptcy petition and £500 on the winding-up petition. The deposit is refundable if the petition is dismissed.

Insolvency proceedings can be an appropriate remedy when all else fails or for recalcitrant debtors where the creditor is sure other enforcement methods will fall on stony ground. Their expense means they are more likely to be employed for higher value claims. It is suggested that creditors contemplating insolvency proceedings consult with a solicitor to determine the way forward.

10.7 Comparative enforcement procedures

Warrant of execution (seizure by county court bailiff of debtor's goods)
Relatively cheap, most straightforward procedure involving no attendance at court, availability against all Defendants. Disadvantage: third party claims.

Writ of Fi Fa (High Court equivalent of warrant)
More expensive and more complex procedure than warrant but still involving no attendance at court, more efficient than warrant, appropriate for larger debts. Disadvantage: third party claims.

Oral examination (obtaining information on Defendant's means)
Not a method of enforcement but a means of identifying further assets which may lead to further enforcement. Cheap, straightforward procedure, may not require attendance at court. Disadvantages: can be slow and ineffectual especially against professional debtors.

Attachment of earnings (instalment payments from Defendant's earnings)
Only available against an employee, not self-employed, cheap, straightforward procedure involving no attendance at court. Disadvantages: slow, Defendant's protected earnings level, more appropriate for smaller debts.

Charging orders (securing debt against Defendant's property)
Does not directly lead to payment but provides a form of security over Defendant's property. More complex procedure involving attendance at court, longer-term solution.

Garnishee orders (obtaining payment from debtor of Defendant)
Cheap, more complex procedure involving attendance at court, timing of service can be crucial.

Bankruptcy petitions (insolvency proceedings against individuals)

Winding-up petitions (insolvency proceedings against companies and firms)
Expensive, complex procedure, involving attendance at court, not available for debts less than £750, usually more appropriate for larger debts.

Request for Warrant of Execution

to be completed and signed by the plaintiff or his solicitor and sent to the court with the appropriate fee

1	Plaintiff's name and address	STAN AND OLLIES (A FIRM) 15 CHUMP STREET OXFORD

In the BRISTOL

County Court

Case Number B 00001

2	Name and address for service and payment (if different from above)	—
	Ref/Tel No.	

For court use only

Warrant no.

Issue date:

Warrant applied for at   o'clock

3	Defendant's name and address	GREENSTREETS LTD, CASABLANCA BUILDING 501 FALLON CRESCENT BRISTOL

Foreign court code/name:

4   Warrant details

I certify that the whole or part of any instalments due under the judgment or order have not been paid and the balance now due is as shown

(A) Balance due at date of this request	3470 : 50
(B) Amount for which warrant to issue	3470 : 50
Issue fee	40 : 00
Solicitor's costs	—
Land Registry fee	—
TOTAL	3510 : 50

Signed *S Laurel*

Plaintiff (Plaintiff's solicitor)

Dated 15/11/95

If the amount of the warrant at (B) is less than the balance at (A), the sum due after the warrant is paid will be

IMPORTANT
You must inform the court immediately of any payments you receive after you have sent this request to the court

Other information that might assist the bailiff including the name(s) and address(es) of any 2nd/3rd defendant and other address(es) at which the defendant might have goods. You should also tell the court if you have reason to believe that the bailiff might encounter serious difficulties in attempting to execute the warrant.

Warrant No.

N323 Request for warrant of execution (Order 26, Rule 1(1))

JORDANS

Jordan and Sons Limited
Jordan and Sons Limited 21 St. Thomas Street, Bristol BS1 6JS. Telephone 0117 923 0600

J/N323   11.91

Request for Oral Examination

to be completed and signed by the plaintiff or his solicitor and sent to the court with the appropriate fee

1 Plaintiff's name and address

FLORENCE NIGHTINGALE,
I SEVASTAPOL ROAD,
LLANELLI

In the

SWANSEA

County Court

Case Number

2 Name and address for service and payment
(if different from above)
Ref/Tel No.

—

For court use only

O/E no.

Issue date:

3 Defendant's name and address

G. GARBO LTD,
NINOCHKA BUILDING,
KARENINA STREET,
SWANSEA.

Hearing date:

on

at   o'clock

4 Name and address of person to be orally examined if different from Box 3

(ie director of defendant company)

G. GARBO (FEMALE)
ADDRESS AS ABOVE

at (address)

5 Judgment details

Court where judgment/order made if not court of issue

LLANELLI

I apply for an order that the above defendant (the officer of the defendant company named in Box 4) attend and be orally examined as to his (the defendant company's) financial circumstances and produce at the examination any relevant books or documents

6 Outstanding debt

*you may be able to claim interest if judgment entered for more than £5000 on or after 1 July 1991

Balance of debt and any interest*/damages at date of this request	1927	00
Issue fee	30	00
AMOUNT NOW DUE	1957	00
Unsatisfied warrant costs	—	

I certify that the balance now due is as shown

Signed *F Nightingale*

Plaintiff (Plaintiff's solicitor)

Dated 26/2/96

IMPORTANT
You must inform the court immediately of any payments you receive after you have sent this request to the court

N316 Request for oral examination (Order 25, rule 3(1A))

JORDANS   Crown Copyright   Reproduced with the permission of the Controller of Her Majesty's Stationery Office
JN316   6.91

Request for Attachment of Earnings Order

to be completed and signed by the plaintiff or his solicitor and sent to the court with the appropriate fee

1 Plaintiff's name and address

HUMPTY DUMPTY LTD,
EGGSHELL BUILDING,
YOLK ROAD,
WALLSEND

In the

YORK

County Court

Case Number Y 1 1 1 2

2 Name and address for service and payment
(if different from above)
Ref/Tel No.

—

For court use only

A / E application no.

Issue date:

Hearing date:

3 Defendant's name and address

JILL JACK,
15 PAIL AVENUE,
TADCASTER

on

at   o'clock

at (address)

4 Judgment details

Court where judgment/order made if not court of issue

—

I apply for an attachment of earnings order

I certify that the whole or part of any instalments due under the judgment or order have not been paid and the balance now due is as shown

5 Outstanding debt

Balance due at date of this request*
(excluding issue fee but including unsatisfied warrant costs)

*you may also be entitled to interest to date of request where judgment is for over £5000 and is entered on or after 1 July 1991

Balance due	750	00
Issue fee	50	00
AMOUNT NOW DUE	800	00

Signed *H. Dumpty*
Plaintiff (Plaintiff's solicitor)

Dated 1/9/94

6 Employment Details *(please give as much information as you can - it will help the court to make an order more quickly)*

Employer's name and address

GRAND OLD DUKE ENTERPRISES,
101 HILL STREET,
YORK

7 Other details
(Give any other details about the defendant's circumstances which may be relevant to the application)

Defendant's place of work
(if different from employer's address)

—

The defendant is employed as   BOOK-KEEPER

Works No / Pay Ref   —

IMPORTANT
You must inform the court immediately of any payments you receive after you have sent this request to the court

N337 Request for attachment of earnings order (Order 27, rule 4(1))   JORDANS

**Form for Replying to an
Attachment of Earnings Application**

- Read the notes on the notice of application before completing this form.

- Tick the correct boxes and give as much information as you can. The court will make an order based on the information you give on this form. You must give full details of your employment and your income and outgoings. Enclose a copy of your most recent pay slip if you can.

- *Make your offer of payment in box 10. You will get some idea of how much to offer by adding up your expenses in boxes 6, 7, 8 and 9 and taking them from your total income (box 5).*

- Send or take this completed and signed form immediately to the court office shown on the notice of application.

- You should keep your copy of the notice of application unless you are making full payment. (This does not apply to maintenance applications).

- For details of where and how to pay see notice of application.

In the	YORK County Court
Case Number	Y1112
Application Number	A/E 999
Plaintiff *(including ref.)*	HUMPTY DUMPTY LTD.
Defendant	JILL JACK

3 Employment

I am ☑ employed as a BOOK-KEEPER

☐ self employed as a

☐ unemployed

☐ a pensioner

a. employment

My employer is GRAND OLD DUKE ENTERPRISES

Employer's address 101 HILL STREET YORK

Address of employer's head office *(if different from above)* —

My works number and/or pay reference is YO1 1JJ

Jobs other than main job *(give details)* —

b. self employment
Length of time self employed ~~years~~ ~~months~~

c. unemployment
Length of time unemployed ~~years~~ ~~months~~

Give details of any outstanding interviews

1 Personal details

Surname JACK

Forename GILLIAN MARY

☐ Mr ☑ Mrs ☐ Miss ☐ Ms

☐ Married ☐ Single ☐ Other *(specify)*

Age 40

Address 15 PAIL AVENUE, TADCASTER

Postcode

2 Dependants *(people you look after financially)*

Number of children in each age group

under 11	11-15	16-17	18 & over
	2		

Other dependants *(give details)*

—

4 Bank account and savings

☑ **I have a bank account**

☐ The account is in credit by . . . £150·00

☐ The account is overdrawn by . . .

☑ **I have a savings or building society account**

The amount in the account is . . . £75·00

N56 Statement of means-attachment of earnings (Order 27, rule 5(1)) (5.95)

5 Income

My usual take home pay *(including overtime, commission, bonuses etc)*	£800·00	per month
My husband's or wife's usual take home pay	£	per
Income support	£	per
Child benefit(s)	£ 20·00	per month
Other state benefit(s)	£	per
My pension(s)	£	per
Others living in my home give me	£	per
Other income *(give details below)*	£	per
	£	per
	£	per
	£	per
Total income	£ 820·00	per month

6 Expenses

(Do not include any payments made by other members of the household out of their own income)
I have regular expenses as follows:

Mortgage *(including second mortgage)*	£180·00	per month
Rent	£	per
Council tax	£ 50·00	per month
Gas	£	per
Electricity	£ 35·00	per month
Water charges	£ 20·00	per month
TV rental and licence	£	per
HP repayments	£	per
Mail order	£	per
Housekeeping, food, school meals	£ 300·00	per month
Travelling expenses	£ 50·00	per month
Children's clothing	£ 40·00	per month
Maintenance payments	£	per
Others *(not court orders or credit debts listed in boxes 8 and 9)*		
	£	per
	£	per
	£	per
Total expenses	£	per

7 Priority debts *(This section is for arrears only. Do not include regular expenses listed in box 6)*

Rent arrears		£	per
Mortgage arrears		£100·00	per month
Council Tax/community charge arrears		£	per
Water charges arrears		£	per
Fuel debts:	Gas	£	per
	Electricity	£	per
	Other	£	per
Maintenance arrears		£	per
Others *(give details below)*			
		£	per
		£	per
Total priority debts		£	per

8 Court orders

Court	Case No. 7511	£25·00	per month
Total court order instalments		£	per

Of the payments above, I am behind with payments to *(please list)*

9 Credit debts

Loans and credit card debts *(please list)*

ACCESS	£35·00	per month
	£	per
	£	per

Of the payments above, I am behind with payments to *(please list)*

10 Offer of Payment

I offer to have £ 20·00 ~~week~~/month deducted from my pay

• If you want an opportunity to pay voluntarily without your employer being ordered to make deductions from your pay you should ask for a suspended order. Tick the box below and give your reasons.

☐ I would like a suspended order because

11 Declaration   I declare that the details I have given above are true to the best of my knowledge

Signed *G. M. Jack*   Dated 30/9/94

Attachment of Earnings Order

To the defendant's employer

STAFF IN CONFIDENCE	
GRAND OLD DUKE ENTERPRISES	

In the	
	YORK **County Court**
Case No. *Always quote this*	YIIII2
Application No	A/E 999
Plaintiff	HUMPTY DUMPTY LTD.
Defendant	JILL JACK
Plaintiff's Ref.	

The defendant who is employed by you at **101 HILL STREET** , **YORK** , as a **BOOK KEEPER** pay ref **Y01 155**, is in arrears under a judgment of the **YORK** County Court and earnings are payable by you to the defendant

You are therefore ordered to make periodical deductions out of the defendant's earnings in accordance with the Attachment of Earnings Act 1971 until £ **825**, the amount payable under the judgment, has been paid.

For the purpose of calculating the deductions

- The normal deduction rate is £ **20** per month
- The protected earnings rate is £ **780** per month

And you are ordered to pay the sums deducted into the office of this court at monthly intervals

Dated:

If you (either the plaintiff or the defendant) object to the terms for payment contained in this order, you must write to the court with your reasons. You have 16 days from the date of the postmark to do this. A hearing will be arranged and you will both be told when to come to court.

Take Notice

To the defendant

This is a copy of an attachment of earnings order sent to your employer

If you change your employer, you must notify the court in writing **within 7 days**, giving the following details:
- the name and address of your new employer (and the pay office if different) • your new rate of pay
- your works number and /or pay reference • the court case number

If you do not do what this notice tells you, you may be fined or imprisoned or both

Defendant's address	Plaintiff's address
JILL JACK 15 PAIL AVENUE TADCASTER	

GLOSSARY OF TERMS

Affidavit	a written declaration of evidence on oath
CCR	County Court Rules 1981
Certificate of judgment	a document certifying judgment obtained from the court
Charging order absolute	a form of security over an asset, usually property, of the Defendant
Charging order nisi	an interim order in this procedure
Circuit judge	a senior judge, whose duties include conducting trials
Defended actions	any proceedings where a Defence to the claim is entered
Defendant	the party against whom proceedings are brought
Deponent	a person swearing an Affidavit
Default Summons	the appropriate summons to issue when seeking a money judgment
District judge	a judge who deals with most interlocutory applications and hears arbitrations and smaller trials
Ex parte	without notice to opposing party
Garnishee	third party owing money to the Defendant
Green Form legal aid	limited legal advice and assistance available to an individual with restricted financial means
Individual voluntary arrangement	an agreement between a debtor and his creditors to repay them in full or in part over a period of time
Interim order	applies to individual voluntary arrangements; prevents, for a period of time, any steps from being taken in proceedings by creditors
Interlocutory	any application before the final hearing of the action
Interpleader	proceedings to determine ownership of goods between a Defendant and a third party
Litigant	a party to the legal proceedings

Plaintiff	the party commencing proceedings
Summary judgment	application for early judgment avoiding full trial
Trustee in bankruptcy	Official Receiver or insolvency practitioner having conduct of a bankrupt individual's affairs
Walking possession agreement	a written agreement entered into with the bailiff by the Defendant not to remove or dispose of goods belonging to it
Writ of Fieri Facias (Fi Fa)	a written order in the High Court to take possession of the Defendant's goods to satisfy judgment (equivalent to county court warrant)

INDEX

References are to paragraph numbers (italic references are to page numbers)